Tailwinds

Tailwinds

The Lore and Language of Fizzles, Farts and Toots

PETER FURZE

MICHAEL O'MARA BOOKS LIMITED

First published in Great Britain in 1998 by
Michael O'Mara Books Limited
9 Lion Yard, Tremadoc Road
London SW4 7NQ

A CIP catalogue record for this book is available
from the British Library

ISBN 1-85479-291-1

1 3 5 7 9 10 8 6 4 2

Designed and typeset by Martin Bristow

Printed and bound in Great Britain
by Caledonian International
Book Manufacturing Limited, Glasgow

Contents

Illustration Acknowledgements

Illustrations copyright © 1998 by Bridgeman Art Library, London: p. 2 (plate 69 of 'Los caprichos', 1799 by Francisco José de Goya y Lucientes); Corbis–Bettmann: pp. 112, 135, 137, 167, 170; Corbis–Bettmann/Reuter: p. 169; Corbis–Bettmann/UPI: pp. 104, 147, 192; Corbis–Hulton Deutsch: p. 98; The Mander & Mitchenson Theatre Collection: p. 138; Mary Evans Picture Library: p. 31; Mary Evans Picture Library/Simon Conti: p. 61; Popperfoto: p. 111; Carole Townsend: p. 129.

Preface and Acknowledgements

THIS LITTLE BOOK is based on a thesis which the late Peter Furze intended to submit in 1996 to the University of Windrush, California, for the degree of Master of Arts. Peter's work was almost complete at the time of his tragic accident. He had even written an Introduction, which follows this Preface. There are some, perhaps, who will find that Introduction rather heavy-going and serious, but it deserves to be read. It is a justification of Peter's work and had much to do with my own decision to prepare *Tailwinds* for publication. I had not, I confess, thought very seriously about farting as an academic subject until I read what Peter had to say, but he convinced me – and I think he will convince others – that it is worthy of attention.

At least one member of faculty had already suggested to Peter (how seriously, I am not too sure) that his forthcoming thesis would be of interest to a wider audience and ought to be published. As far as I know, Peter was in favour of that idea, and would have been glad to see it appear in this form. Peter's own working title for his thesis, incidentally, which he thought might need expanding in order to make it more specific, was *A Linguistic, Literary, Social, Cultural, Biological and Medical Study of Flatulence and its Consequences from the Classical Period to Modern Times, with Observations on the Physical and Psychological Damage caused by Perdological Repression and Notes about the Subject as an Inspiration for Mainly Coarse Humour in Prose and Verse*. I'm afraid that the title I have used instead, namely *Tailwinds*, would have struck Peter as being too vague, and perhaps not solemn enough, but it is certainly easier to fit on to a title page.

The five years of research in which Peter was able to immerse himself would not have been possible but for a generous grant from the International Institute of Baked Bean Canners. I know he would have wanted me to take this opportunity of publicly thanking the administrators of the Institute's Educational Foundation for their support.

I wish I could say that those of us who were Peter's contemporaries at Windrush University also deserved thanks, but it must unfortunately be said that when we 'got wind' of his thesis subject, as we inevitably expressed it, our continued references to the 'Master of Farts' degree on which he was working were probably not very helpful. Nor was he assisted by the nation-wide media interest that forced him to go into hiding for several months after a member of the student body, whose identity remained unknown to him to the last, misrepresented to a local television station the subject of his thesis. I still feel guilty about that, and hope that the work I have done to prepare *Tailwinds* for the press partly makes up for it.

Peter was probably the most thorough graduate-researcher ever seen at Windrush. He sought confirmation for everything, and it was typical of him that although he was not a scientist, he experimented in the laboratory with his self-produced methane to see whether it really would explode under certain conditions. Unhappily for him, it did. RIP Peter Furze.

Tailwinds, then, is mostly based on Peter's thesis, but much work remained to be done after his tragic accident if it was to appear in print. I was obliged for practical reasons to reduce the 700 pages of typescript that Peter had already produced to something of more manageable size. Perhaps while summarizing his work I have also allowed my own less serious attitude to the subject to make itself apparent, though I tried to reflect Peter's view that the lore and language of flatulence deserve the greatest respect. I doubt whether anyone has ever taken a fart as seriously as Peter Furze. It became one of his aims in life to add status to flatus, as it were. By contrast, I must confess with some shame that, in me, the whole subject of flatulence tends to appeal to a sense of humour that has remained at adolescent level. This is unfortunate, but at least my efforts have enabled the essence of Peter's work to reach the public it deserves – and, in spite of my editing and occasional light-hearted additions, the odour of Peter Furze, if one may so express it, still lingers within the pages of *Tailwinds*.

I became aware of some of the difficulties Peter faced while gathering his materials when I attempted to seek further information about some of his entries. I soon discovered that it is by no means easy to approach strangers and ask them about farting. I tried asking one or two people to say which 'fart' euphemisms and synonyms they used, but even when they were professional linguists who might have been expected to respond objectively, the response was sometimes very negative. The sniffy comment that 'talking about farting is not one of my strong points' was the only contribution I could obtain from a Professor of Linguistics in one Canadian university, for example. Several other academics ignored requests for help, and even in their silence one could somehow sense their disapproval, but as Mark Twain said: 'To the unconsciously indelicate all things are delicate.' That great writer made another comment relevant to this work when he said: 'It is not the word that is the sin, it is the spirit back of the word.'

As one who has only dabbled in this area of research, I now have much sympathy for those who professionally try to investigate slang and euphemisms. By their very nature these areas of language usually deal with taboo subjects, but they deserve scholarly investigation. For dedicated researchers like Peter Furze, help from competent informants will always be essential. In retrospect I see that Peter must often have had a difficult time as he sought the academic help he needed.

Peter seemed to become more and more dejected, in fact, as those he tried to question about the passing of anal gas responded impolitely or not at all. I remember thinking that for some time he had looked decidedly down in the dumps. There are even those amongst Peter's acquaintances – he had few friends (no friends, now I think of it, though I knew him fairly well because we happened to be two British students at the same American university) – who believe that the fart-methane explosion which ended his life was no accident.

Several people were heard to mutter phrases like 'the balance of his mind was disturbed', arguing that anyone who spent five years of his life studying farts *must* be crazy. The coroner, however, recorded a verdict of accidental death, not suicide, and there the matter must rest. I personally console myself with the thought that, accident or not, Peter died as he would have wished, in the middle of a fart investigation.

The unhelpful response from some quarters to questions about rectal exhalations made the positive contributions of others even more significant. It is therefore with special sincerity that I acknowledge, on Peter Furze's behalf as well as my own, the help of the following correspondents. Without their contributions, *Tailwinds* would never have seen the light of day.

Australian contributions of great interest were forwarded by Helen Vnuk and Dann Lennard, who in turn gathered many of them from their friends and colleagues. Joan Houston Hall, associate editor of the *Dictionary of American Regional English*, was a generous supplier of materials. Paul J. Dine, Terrence Keough, Charles Boewe and Donald M. Lance made wide-ranging and frequent comments of great usefulness. Others whose e-mail messages from various parts of the English-speaking world provided information and support were George H. Scheetz, William King, Susan Whitebook, Jack Chambers, Peggy Smith (and the students of her Public Speaking and Debate class at Cleveland Heights High School, Ohio), Daniel Long, Gene Marquis, Lisa Hoyman, Sheila Embleton, Katie Wales, Bob Marsden, Dave Henson, Paul Townsend, Edwin Moore, Randy Roberts, Cleveland Evans, Roger Owen, Ken Tucker, Grant Smith, Philip L. Taylor, Douglas McNair Taylor, Gay Wilson, Daniel McKinley, Mike Shupp, Gordon Wright. Other contributors are named in relevant entries. As an old saying has it (or if it doesn't, it should): 'May they fart with ease, and their odours please.'

Fartyewell,
Hubert Allen
106407.3560@compuserve.com

Introduction

ONE OF THE MOST NATURAL and necessary human activities, performed several times a day, involves the release through the anus of the excessive gas, or flatus, which builds up within the digestive system. In other words, we all need to fart. That simpler statement of the situation will immediately be condemned by those who consider the word 'fart' to be distasteful, a rude word which must be banned from polite conversation and respectable publications. If reference must be made at all to such a topic, such critics would argue, then it should at least be disguised as 'breaking wind', 'passing gas', 'tooting', 'trumping', or hidden beneath a similar euphemism. As we shall see, there are plenty of such euphemistic synonyms available in the English language; some 350 of them are mentioned in the pages that follow.

Let us pause for a moment to ask why 'fart' was outlawed from polite conversation in the first place. At one time it was a normal word, used with no suggestion of embarrassment. In the thirteenth and fourteenth centuries this everyday activity was freely discussed at court, and at all lower social levels. The subject itself gave rise to a great deal of hearty laughter, as the works of Geoffrey Chaucer reveal. It was in the centuries which followed that different codes of behaviour and speech began to separate the social classes, while the more evangelical varieties of Protestantism began to make their influence felt. Where Roman Catholics were deeply offended by blasphemy, the Puritans seem to have been more deeply upset by what they considered to be obscenity. As a typical seventeenth-century playwright, Shakespeare made fun of Puritanism, but he felt its effects. He was obviously aware of the word 'fart', yet he makes no use of it in his plays, even to please the groundlings. At one point he allows an actor to say 'fartuous' where 'virtuous' is meant, and he alludes to the breaking of wind, but he goes no further. He is 'watching his language', and nowhere in his plays does he exploit the comic potential of a farting scene.

From Shakespeare's time onwards, what was considered to be the language of the streets was spurned by those who could make use of an artificially polite, literary English. It is no coincidence that it is in the mid-seventeenth century that the first references in English to 'euphemisms' occur. Euphemistic words and phrases had long been in use, but now there was a conscious awareness of them and they were duly labelled. These ridiculous words, with all their attendant hypocrisy, have flourished ever since. From the eighteenth century onwards, an artificial delicacy with regard to language and social behaviour grew steadily more marked. Jonathan Swift was among those who laughed at its worst excesses, but to no avail. It reached its most absurd level in nineteenth-century middle-class society, when it temporarily became impossible to refer to parts of the body in mixed company. If chicken was

served to dinner-guests, a 'leg' had to be referred to as a 'drumstick'; a request for some 'white meat' managed to avoid the highly embarrassing word 'breast'. A man's trousers at this time were his 'unmentionables', and so it went on.

In one respect it would seem as if these absurdities were thankfully behind us, since there has been in modern times a relaxation of attitudes. Some might even say that we have relaxed too much, as we are now regularly exposed to words in the media which would have led to legal action only a generation ago. We now live in a world where the four-letter 'eff' word can commonly be heard and read.

That four-letter 'eff' word, needless to say, is not 'fart', which probably receives less media exposure, and remains less used in ordinary conversation, than the 'eff' word itself. Here is a recent comment on the subject by Gwen Foor, writing in the *Northern Michigan Journal*: 'Breaking wind! Otherwise known as flatulence, gas or that other little four-letter word, the one that starts with "f", ends with "t" and makes anyone under 14 or so giggle and anyone over 14 or so slap one stiff hand over their mouth, raise their eyes to the ceiling as they take in a sudden deep breath and exclaim, "Oh, my!" Fainting is even an approved option for the seriously stuffy types.'

Of course this is an exaggeration, but few would deny that middle-class Americans remain seriously uptight about the use of 'fart'. In Britain there are signs of relaxation, but mainstream comedy programmes still tend to allude to flatulence rather than refer directly to farting. In a typical episode of the BBC television series *Birds of a Feather*, for example, there was a dialogue in which someone referred to dropping a glass. The comment was then made: '*You'd* better not drop one,' with the *double entendre* clearly intended. In the same episode a man who had eaten a lot of garlic remarked: 'I'll be lifting the blankets tonight.' The word 'fart' itself was used only when two people were described as 'old farts'.

The reluctance in all English-speaking countries to use 'fart' in its primary sense defies logical explanation. Surely it is time for the word to be welcomed back into our normal vocabulary, from which it should never have been banished in the first place. We could perhaps also restore some of the words like 'fizzle',' 'fyst' and 'trump', which formerly distinguished types of fart. Beyond these purely linguistic considerations, it is also time for us to learn from our ancestors how to be more relaxed about this natural phenomenon, the breaking of wind from the anus. Every child instinctively knows, before adult inhibitions are imposed on it, that these bodily noises and smells are funny. It should stay that way.

This thesis began as a linguistic study of slang and euphemisms, but it has insisted on adding to itself an account of what can only be called 'farting lore'. A reasonable number of jokes, verses and anecdotes related to the subject have therefore been included, though the coarser examples of the genre, which regrettably are to be found in great numbers, have been omitted. The work has also become a miniature dictionary of relevant quotations, with its contributions from, among others, Aristophanes, Saint Augustine, Chaucer, Jonson, Suckling, Sterne, and Benjamin Franklin, not to mention contemporary authors such as John Updike, Norman Mailer, Bernard Malamud, Henry Miller and Philip Roth. The better writers, the most linguistically sensitive people of their time, have never had a problem about mentioning farts and farting. It is time that we learned from their example.

PETER FURZE

Abu Hasan's breaking of wind
....

The story of Abu Hasan appears in *The Book of the Thousand Nights and a Night*, otherwise known as the *Arabian Nights Entertainments*. Sir Richard Burton's translation of this classic was privately printed by the Burton Club, 1885. His version of Abu Hasan's story can be summarized as follows:

Abu Hasan was an opulent merchant. His wife died when both were still young, and his friends urged him to marry again. Abu Hasan duly entered into negotiations with the old women who arrange matches, and married a maid of great beauty. The wedding banquet was a great celebration, and everyone was invited. 'The whole house was thrown open to feasting: there were rices of five different colours, and sherbets of as many more; and kid goats stuffed with walnuts, almonds, and

pistachios; and a young camel roasted whole. So they ate and drank and made mirth and merriment; and the bride was displayed in her seven dresses.'

Eventually the bridegroom was summoned to the chamber where his bride sat enthroned, and he rose slowly and with dignity from his divan; but as he did so, 'because he was over-full of meat and drink, lo and behold! he brake wind, great and terrible. Thereupon each guest turned to his neighbour and talked aloud, and made as though he had heard nothing.' Abu Hasan, however, was terribly embarrassed. Instead of going to the bridal chamber he went down to the courtyard, saddled his horse and rode off, weeping bitterly.

In time he reached Lahej, where he boarded a ship about to sail to India. There he remained for ten years, but at the end of that time 'he was seized with homesickness, and the longing to behold his native land was that of a lover pining for his beloved; and he came near to die of yearning desire.' Abu Hasan returned secretly to his native land, disguised in rags. 'But when he drew near his old home, he looked down upon it from the hills with brimming eyes, and said to himself, "There is a chance that they might know thee; so I will wander about the outskirts and hearken to the folk. Allah grant that what happened to me be not remembered by them."

'He listened carefully for seven nights and seven days, till it so chanced that, as he was sitting at the door of a hut, he heard the voice of a young girl saying, "O my mother, tell me the day when I was born, for one of my companions is about to tell my fortune." And the mother answered, "Thou wast born, O my daughter, on the very night when Abu Hasan brake wind."'

When Abu Hasan heard these words 'he rose up from the bench and fled away, saying to himself, "Verily thy breaking of wind hath become a date, which shall last for ever and ever."' He returned to India and remained in exile for the rest of his life.

For a similar tale of an Englishman's self-exile because of a fart, see *Embarrassing moments*.

Accident

A euphemism for 'fart' in occasional modern use, as in 'Oops – sorry about that – a little accident!' Eric Partridge, in his *Dictionary of Historical Slang*, says that 'accident' has also been used since the end of the nineteenth century 'for any untimely, or accidental, call of nature'.

Acoustic considerations

The prevailing acoustic affects a noisy emission of anal gas as much as any other sound. The average toilet bowl, for example, can act as an echo-chamber which enables a modest escape to be heard throughout the house. However, musical quality, as well as the sheer noise, can be affected. Speaking of King's College Chapel, Cambridge, David Willcocks once remarked: 'It's the building. That acoustic would make a fart sound like a sevenfold Amen.' It is not known how many choir boys, who delight in literal interpretations of metaphors when it suits them, have put these words to the test. Too many, one suspects, for the liking of the College authorities.

Affcot

This is defined by Douglas Adams and John Lloyd in *The Meaning of Liff* as 'the sort of fart you hope people will talk after'. They make a useful point. Nothing is worse than a backfire which interrupts a conversation and leads to a sudden astonished silence. See also *Berepper* and *Brompton*.

African sayings

An article in the magazine *Maledicta*, volume 11, entitled 'Obscenity and Vulgarity in African Oral Folklore', by J. Olowo Ojoade, mentions some sayings based on the breaking of wind. Examples are:

'The dog says: "There is nothing that can be eaten in a fart."' (Ilaje and Yoruba) The meaning is the same as that expressed by the Latin tag *ex nihilo nihil fit*, 'out of nothing nothing comes'.

'The hungry man will not laugh when the server of food farts.' (Fulani) In other words, a person may not react in the usual way to a particular stimulus if there is something more pressing on his mind.

'If your body stinks, people in your company take the opportunity to fart.' (Akan) This means that if you are well known to be a thief, for example, your neighbours will steal when you are around, believing that you will come under suspicion.

'It is the fart of a poor person that smells; when a rich person farts, people say, "Ease for my anus, my lord."' (Edo) Or as we might say in English: 'One law for the rich, another for the poor.' Variants of this saying include 'A chief's fart does not have an evil smell.' (Nembe) 'The white man does not fart.' (Hausa) The last of these is presumably an ironic comment, meaning that he never admits to it. See also *Non-farters, the*.

Afterburner
....

Technically this describes an emission which has a high methane content and can therefore be set alight. Producing such an exhalation in front of a naked flame is referred to by some of those who practise the art as 'pyroflatulating.'

Air
....

Frequently used with reference to breaking wind, in expressions like 'I was just expelling/dispelling/tearing/exhausting/passing air,' or 'I was taking an air dump.' George H. Scheetz mentions another possibility: 'I am not sure how my ex-wife, children, and I came up with our particular euphemism, "to have air", but we have used this terminology for nearly a decade. My own sister, on a visit with her family over the Christmas holiday, did not know what I meant when I used the phrase.'

A slightly more elaborate term, used in both North America and Australia, is 'air cake' or 'air biscuit', as in 'someone's floated an air biscuit.' In Britain, 'air' tends to be used by those who have been exposed to someone else's unpleasant smell, in an utterance such as 'Give me air!' Gwen Foor also uses the word punningly when writing about attitudes to flatulence in the *Northern Michigan Journal*: 'Our discomfort as a society with such a natural occurrence intrigues me. As a preschool and kindergarten teacher, it is a behaviour that airs itself, so to speak, on a weekly, if not daily basis in the classroom.'

All fart and no shit

Royal Navy slang used to describe a noisy but ineffective leader.

Always let your wind go free

This piece of folk-wisdom is almost proverbial and is likely to be quoted in justification by a man who breaks wind in the presence of other people. The source of the saying is not known, though there is said to be a gravestone epitaph somewhere in Britain which reads:

> Wheresoever you may be,
> Always let your wind go free.
> I held mine and it done for me.
> R.I.P.

This is not quite as ridiculous as it might seem; the failure to expel intestinal gas can certainly have severe consequences for the person concerned. The American version of this saying runs: 'Let your gas [or air] go free wherever you may be.'

The basic philosophy encapsulated in the saying is not recent, nor is it confined to the western world. It would be tempting to cite Khushwant Singh in support of this comment, since he writes in *Delhi, a Novel*: 'Verily hath Shaikh Saadi said:

> O Sage! the stomach is the prison house of wind,
> The sagacious contain it not in captivity,

If wind torment thy belly, release it, fart;
For the wind in the stomach is like a stone
on the heart.'

However, this is no doubt only a parody of Saadi, a poet known for his extravagant metaphors and flamboyant images. Nor is it likely that there existed, other than in Singh's imagination, the Greek Niarchos who supposedly wrote in the first century AD:

If blocked, a fart can kill a man;
If let escape, a fart can sing
Health giving songs; farts kill and save.
A fart is a powerful king.

By contrast we can be sure that in the eleventh century the School of Salerno had a Health Code which included the passage: 'To expel certain winds is considered almost a crime, yet those who suppress them risk dropsy, convulsions, vertigo and colic.' Boorde's *Dietary* (1542) also specifically says: 'Make no restriction of wind and water, nor siege [prevent from emerging] what nature would expel.'

Anal cork, the

James Joyce conjures up the interesting image of the anal cork in *Ulysses* (1922). He writes: 'He uncorks himself behind: then, contorting his features, farts loudly. Take that! He recorks himself.' For a comment on the 'Take that!' see *Perdological Salutations*. Robert Marsden reports that when he was camped in his youth with the Boys' Brigade, a cork was always ceremoniously presented to the boy who ate most prunes, on the assumption that he would soon be passing quantities of gas.

Anal vapour

A reference to the supposed mist that is produced by a wet-sounding emission, known in slang as 'a wet one'.

Angelic farting

In *Angela's Ashes*, by Frank McCourt, the young hero knows that there are rules about when it is permissible or not to use the word 'fart' in conversation. He talks to the Angel on the Seventh Step of their house, because that is where his father has told him the Angel comes to deliver his younger brothers and sisters. Frankie says: 'That's the way I'd like to be in the world, a gas man, not giving a fiddler's fart, and that's what I tell the Angel on the Seventh Step till I remember you're not supposed to say fart in the presence of an angel.'

Anxiety

A person who is feeling tense or anxious is likely to pass more wind than usual. Scientists accept that this is so, but are as yet unable to explain why it happens. It is possible that anxiety causes an individual to swallow more air, which then has to be expelled.

Aristocratic wind-breaking

British aristocrats have long had a reputation amongst Americans for eccentric behaviour. It is thought that the aristocrats take no heed of normal social conventions. A well-known joke that circulates in the US is based on the belief that the members of the nobility are willing to break wind loudly whenever the need arises, regardless of circumstances. The aristocrats themselves, according to received opinion, show no embarrassment, though their non-aristocratic guests may be embarrassed on their behalf and feel obliged to camouflage their action.

In one version of this story, two very English Englishmen and one American are having dinner with Lord So-and-so. When his lordship 'forgets himself', one of the Englishmen immediately takes responsibility for the explosion and makes his excuses. When it happens a second time, the other Englishman pretends that he was the guilty party and says 'Excuse me!' A little later his lordship breaks wind yet again.

The American, much amused, immediately says: 'No, gentlemen, I absolutely insist. This one's on me.'

In a less convincing version of this tale, it is three American GIs who are being served tea in a duchess's parlour at the end of World War Two. One of the GIs says 'Pardon me,' when the duchess trumpets mightily. When she does this again, the second GI says, 'Excuse me.' At the third instance, the remaining GI quickly raises his hand to say: 'No, fellas, this one's on me.'

Mike Shupp, writing from California, adds one or two refinements. He has the English male guests rising in turn after the eruptions of a duchess 'to bow slightly to the group and murmur, "Terribly sorry." It is quietly explained to the American guest that 'it wouldn't be proper for a lady to admit to breaking wind.' He therefore cheerfully stands up to accept responsibility on the third occasion.

The standing up and bowing may have been influenced by what was perhaps the original form of the joke, which circulates in Germany under yet another disguise. It is used there to make a different point altogether. In the German version it is Queen Victoria who loudly passes gas in the presence of several ambassadors. The French ambassador voluntarily takes the blame for the first royal mishap; the English ambassador accepts responsibility for the second. On the third occasion the German ambassador decides to assert the superiority of his country. He clicks his heels and bows, then announces that on behalf of the Kaiser he takes responsibility for 'this one and the next three'.

Aristophanes

There are many down-to-earth references to flatulence in the comic plays of Aristophanes, but as *The Oxford Companion to Classical Literature* says: 'his indecency is coarse and outspoken but not prurient or morbid.' There is a typical exchange in *The Knights*, which dates from 420 BC. The Sausage Seller asks Demos: 'Do you remember the time when silphium [a Mediterranean plant, used as a condiment] was so cheap?' 'Aye, to be sure I do!' 'Very well! It was Cleon who had caused the price to fall so low, that all might eat it, and the jurymen in the Courts were almost asphyxiated from farting in each other's faces.' 'Hah! Why, indeed, a Dungtownite told me the same thing.' 'Were you not yourself in those days quite red in the gills with farting?'

Arty-farty

A description of something or someone who is pretentiously artistic. The '-farty' part of the word was clearly used originally for the sake of the rhyme, but it manages to cancel out very effectively any suggestion of superiority that 'arty' might convey. 'Arty-crafty' is a milder form of the expression. 'Artsy-fartsy' and 'artsy-craftsy' are also found.

As much use as a fart in a wind tunnel

This expression occurs in *The Touch of Innocents*, a novel by Michael Dobbs. The chairman of a business meeting tells his colleagues: 'You know that the MP-Double-A means everything to this company. Without it we're about as much use as a fart in a wind tunnel.' This rather implies that in other circumstances a fart can be decidedly useful, as perhaps it can – see *Useful farts*.

The variant 'as much chance as a fart in a windstorm' is quoted as an American saying in a *Dictionary of Popular Phrases*, by Nigel Rees, and as a Canadian expression by Eric Partridge in his *Dictionary of Slang*. Presumably this was what

Michael Dobbs's chairman meant – that without a key product the company would stand as little chance of surviving as a fart in a windstorm. Bill King reports from Arizona on yet another version of this saying, used by one of his West Virginia relatives: 'He's as worthless as a fart in a whirlwind.' Roy Wilder, in *You All Spoken Here*, says that another phrase of much the same meaning, also used in the American South, is 'like a popcorn fart in hell'. 'Like a fart in a gale/windstorm/thunderstorm' can also be said of someone whose actions are considered to be ineffective.

Asses
······

The comment that asses are notorious farters becomes rather ambiguous in American English, where 'ass' is the usual form of British 'arse'. But the asses in this instance are otherwise known as donkeys, possibly the loudest breakers of wind in the animal kingdom. Some of the blame for this can be levelled at their vegetable diet, which may include down thistle, or *Onopordon acanthium*. In his seventeenth-century translation of Pliny, Philemon Holland writes: 'As for Onopordon, they say if asses eat thereof, they will fall a fizzling and farting.' This is being kind to the donkeys, since 'fizzling' refers to quiet emissions – rarely the case where donkeys are concerned.

There is a limerick which makes use of the ambiguity in American English of the word 'ass'. It runs as follows:

> There was a young maid from Madras
> Who had a magnificent ass;
>   Not rounded and pink,
>   As you probably think –
> It was grey, had long ears, and ate grass.

At sparrow-fart

This dialectal expression means 'very early in the morning, at dawn.'

Backfire

This comments on a loud anal explosion in expressions like 'Somebody just backfired.' The culprit himself may remark 'That's one that backfired.' A similar term is 'back-talk'.

Barking spider

Used for a breaking of wind by or to young American children, as in 'Did I hear a barking spider?' or 'Those barking spiders are back again.' Tim Rogers, in an article called 'Rearing', says that his father 'taught me at an early age about the elusive species of arachnid known as the barking spider'. This expression no doubt began when adults needed to find an answer to the child's question – 'What was that noise, daddy?' An alternative answer is: 'A spider bark'. 'Bark' itself is sometimes used as a synonym for the kind of anal emission which is a sharp report.

Baseball caps

Baseball caps with 'fart' or 'old fart' slogans are readily available in novelty shops. Typical slogans on the caps include 'Hoof Arted', 'Old Farts Need Love Too', 'Old Farts Never Die. They Just Lose Their Wind'. Such caps have not yet become an item of high fashion, gracing the cat-walks. They tend to be worn by men of a certain age out on a drinking spree.

Beans

Beans have long been associated with flatulence, and with good reason. As with other legumes, beans are likely to increase the amount of flatus that accumulates in the body and needs to be expelled. (See also *Flatulence*.) An early reference to the subject is found in the writings of Saint Jerome. He forbade his nuns to eat beans, believing that *in partibus genitalibus titillationes producunt*, 'they tickle the genitals', presumably as wind passes by them. An English text of 1576 remarks that 'beans are naturally more windy than barley.'

In more modern times the 'baked bean blast' is a well-known phenomenon throughout the western world, following a meal where such beans have been consumed. As one correspondent graphically expressed it: 'big bowls of lentils lead to enough farts from the butt of one vegetarian to fill every balloon in the circus.' (In reality, the average man releases enough flatus in a day to blow up one small balloon.) The same informant mentioned that 'my mother used the term "bean noise", as in "who made a bean noise"?' A similar term is 'beanie', as in 'do your beanies always smell that bad?'

Strictly speaking it is not the beans themselves that cause flatulence, but the human inability to digest them properly. Beans contain the complex carbohydrates raffinose and stachyose, and the enzymes necessary to digest these sugars do not exist in humans. That task is therefore left to certain harmless bacteria which live in the intestines.

In Michael Rumaker's story *The Desert*, there is a scene where a group of hoboes are about to eat a bean-based meal. The dialogue runs: '"My belly's got the windjams, it's that empty." "Beans'll push it down a cave or two." "I'll play you some after dinner music." "A treat to my ears." "We'll shoot perfume around."' This vaguely recalls the flatulent calliope-effect episode in *Blazing Saddles*, the 1974 wild-west parody with Mel Brooks and Richard Pryor. This is a movie which everyone seems to remember because of that one scene.

As it happens, the gas potential of beans can be considerably reduced by soaking them and then discarding the water before cooking. There is also an over-the-counter product available in America called Beano, an enzyme which allows better digestion of foods such as beans and thus cuts down on the amount of flatus and disconcerting sound effects normally produced. About five drops of the liquid are added to the first mouthful of an offending food – and the enzyme does the rest.

In Britain the word 'beano', meaning a spree, derives from 'bean-feast', the term used in the nineteenth century for the annual dinner given by benevolent employers to their employees. One imagines that these occasions were rather windy affairs. Perhaps life on board a Royal Navy ship was formerly smelly for a similar reason. Haricot beans (known as navy beans in the USA) were used as a substitute for potatoes, giving rise to the saying: 'The navy runs on beans.'

To be 'full of beans' has no flatulent associations in English, where it simply means 'lively and cheerful'. The original allusion was to bean-fed horses. The connection is made in French, where 'to be full of beans' is *péter du feu* or *péter des flammes*, literally 'to fart fire' or 'to fart flames'. See also *Snappers*.

Beavis and Butt-Head

These cartoon characters can be relied upon to bring flatulent humour down to the lowest level, which largely accounts for their great popularity. In an episode called 'Atomic Butt Blast', written by Christopher E. Forman, Butt-Head eats several burritos for lunch. In class a little later he explains to his teacher: 'Now I have to fart!' In case Mr Buzzcut has failed to get the point, the boys elaborate: 'Blow a gas-ket. Let one rip. Squeak a breeze. Step on a duck. Pass gas out your ass! Unleash an atomic butt blast!' Several hours later, when Butt-Head eventually manages to pass gas, they comment: 'That was a mega-fart! That was an uncorked symphony! That was a Mighty Morphin' Power Rauncher!'

Beef

A slang word for 'fart', presumably from the rhyming slang expression 'beef-heart'. It is used, for example, by L. Collingwood in his short story *Blue Angel*, which he makes available on the Internet. He speaks about young boys revelling in the 'mystery and magic of their own bodies', and adds: 'I never met one yet who didn't thrill to the music of his own flatulence. Simply consider for a moment the vocabulary created to celebrate the process. There's farting, tooting, breaking wind, beefing, queefing and cutting cheese. There's laying a big one and letting her rip and the ever popular call of "low flying geese".'

'Queef' has not been found in any other context, but it is noticeable of this group of euphemisms that they are often used within the confines of a small group, such as a single family.

Belch

A 'belch' is simply another way of breaking wind. Some speakers therefore use 'belch' itself as a synonym, or euphemism, for 'fart'. Those who accept that this is stretching the meaning of 'belch' overmuch may nevertheless speak of a 'belch in reverse', 'a belch that's gone astray' or 'a belch upside down'. The reverse process leads to a belch being referred to in slang as a 'mouth fart'. See also *Bottom burp*.

Bending down

An action that can be fraught with danger, likely to encourage a breaking of wind at the wrong moment. Weight-lifters and those who practise martial arts are said to be especially prone to untimely escapes. See also *Embarrassing moments* and *Feminine toots*.

Benefit of Farting Explain'd, The

The tenth edition of a pamphlet bearing this title was published in 1722. Eric Partridge saw a copy listed in a bookseller's catalogue but was too late to purchase it. It had supposedly been written in Spanish by Don Fart in Hando and translated by Obadiah Fizzle.

Berepper

One of the place names converted to a word and assigned a definition in *The Meaning of Liff*, by Douglas Adams and John Lloyd. In this instance Berepper (Cornwall) became 'the irrevocable and sturdy fart released in the presence of royalty, which sounds like a small motorbike passing by (but not enough to be confused with one)'. For details of a berepper released in the presence of Elizabeth I, see *Embarrassing moments*.

Biblical references

The Club Methane site on the Web claims to have found a biblical reference to flatulence in the Old Testament,

Jeremiah 4:19. The King James text has: 'My bowels, my bowels! I am pained at my very heart; my heart maketh a noise in me; I cannot hold my peace, because thou hast heard, O my soul, the sound of the trumpet, the alarm of war.' The Revised Standard Version translates this passage rather differently: 'My anguish, my anguish! I writhe in pain! Oh, the walls of my heart! My heart is beating wildly; I cannot keep silent; for I hear the sound of the trumpet, the alarm of war.'

Lamentations 1:20 in the Authorized Version has: 'Behold, O Lord; for I am in distress: my bowels are troubled; mine heart is turned within me.' In the Revised Standard this becomes: 'Behold, O Lord, for I am in distress, my soul is in tumult, my heart is wrung within me.'

The problem is that, for the modern reader, 'bowels' are associated only with the idea of bodily waste matter, with 'emptying one's bowels', 'bowel movements', and the like. When the Authorized Version of the Bible first appeared, 'bowels' also had several other meanings which were subsequently lost. The word could refer simply to the innermost part of the body, or to the womb, or metaphorically to the seat of emotions such as pity. A seventeeth-century reader of the Bible would have understood 'my bowels are troubled' to mean 'my soul is in tumult', as the modern translation has it.

Blaming the dog

The ladies of high society who first began to insist that their lap-dogs should accompany them everywhere were perhaps genuine dog-lovers. It is just as likely, however, that they recognized the convenience of being able to blame the dog when a foul smell made itself apparent in their vicinity. Timothy Kendall was already saying as much in his *Flowers of Epigrammes* (1577): 'She would not misse her fistyng curre [would not be without her farting dog] for any thyng: and why? Forsothe when so she letts a scape, she cries me, fie curre, fie.' 'Fisting-dog' (see Fyst) seems to have been a term as much in use as 'lap-dog' in former centuries. Randle Holme, in *The*

Academy of Armory (1688), says that a dog of this kind was 'such as Ladies delight in'.

The situation had not changed by the eighteenth century. In the second edition of *A Classical Dictionary of the Vulgar Tongue*, Francis Grose defined 'fice or foyse' as 'a small windy escape backwards, more obvious to the nose than ears'. He then made a point of adding: 'frequently by old ladies charged on their lap-dogs'. 'Lap-dogs', in other words, maintained their role as 'taking-the-rap-dogs'.

Dogs certainly do suffer from flatulence, in both senses of the word 'suffer'. They have a much greater sensitivity to smell than humans and probably do not enjoy gas escapes from their owners. Their own flatus is also often especially smelly. Women have been known to say that it is one of the things that dogs have in common with men, along with taking up too much room in bed, having an irrational fear of a vacuum-cleaner, and so on. Breeds that are brachycephalic (with compressed noses) are thought to swallow more air when eating than other dogs, which in turn makes them windier. Two dogs fed from the same bowl will also tend to swallow excessive air, because they will rush to gulp down their food.

Individual dogs react in different ways when they flatulate. Dog-owners report that there are those who are noisy about it, and then chase their tails as if they want to catch the sound. Others manage to look reproachfully at one of the people in the room, causing anyone else who is present to think that the dog is indicating the culprit. Some dogs are clearly pleased with themselves and wag their tails, and at least one owner has sworn that his dog smiles when he (the dog) breaks wind.

Sensible dogs do nothing that will attract attention to themselves at what the American company AkPharma refers to in its sales literature as 'those dreadful moments in the living

room when you don't know whether to look at each other or the dog'. The company markets a product called 'Curtail' which reduces canine flatulence. However, although dogs really are on occasion responsible for a nasty smell, if dogs had the power of speech they would frequently be raising their paws to say 'not guilty' when falsely accused. As it is, in many a dog-owning household there are pets who can do no more than cast a reproachful look at the true offender when someone says the modern equivalent of 'Fie, curre! Fie!'

Sometimes the dog does manage to have the last laugh. Dave Miles has written of an embarrassing trip in an airliner, during which his family poodle was tucked under the seat in a bag. The dog was suffering from flatulence throughout the flight, as many passengers noticed. Since the dog could not be seen, many hostile looks were directed at Dave Miles himself. It was a rare instance of a man being obliged to take the blame for his dog. See also *Crab* and *Redneck definition*.

Blanket ripper

Used to describe an anal explosion which takes place beneath the blankets, ideally when the perpetrator is alone in bed. The masochist then puts his head under the clothes to appreciate the smell. A sadist insists that his partner, if one happens to be present, does the smelling. See also *Dutch oven*.

Blast

A word frequently used in connection with flatulence, in its blast of wind sense. A 'fart', in slang, is sometimes a 'blast', 'butt blast' or 'hinder-blast', while an Australian correspondent reports that her partner is likely to enter an office saying, 'Wait for it, wait for it,' before 'blasting away'. A man who is especially known for passing gas is sometimes referred to as a 'master blaster'. In a different context, W. Buchan reported in his book *Domestic Medicine* (1845) that 'country people call this flatulent disease in sheep a blast, and imagine it proceeds from foul air, or ill wind.'

Bleep

Used as a euphemism for 'fart', for example, by the American feminist Andrea Dworkin in her writings. Since a bleep is usually the sound that is substituted for a rude word in radio or television programmes, it seems especially apt to use the word 'bleep' as a substitute for a taboo word.

Blockbuster

A word sometimes used to describe a very loud anal explosion. A 'blockbuster' was originally a large high-explosive bomb used for demolition purposes, though it now tends to be used of a sensational film, book, etc., that is expected to make a lot of money.

Blow off

A British and Australian euphemism for 'fart', especially amongst schoolchildren. *The Kenneth Williams Diaries*, edited by Russell Davies, has an entry for 3 June, 1963: 'At 6.45 we had the cocktail party with the Captain. Handshakes and bonhomie. Me blowing off very liberally.' It is noticeable that in later years Williams abandoned this schoolboy phrase in favour of the more direct 'farting'.

Similar terms used in this context include 'blow, big blow, blow one's wind, blow off steam, blowout, blow a gasket, blow it up, deal the blow, blow the horn, blow your horn'. 'Bugling' also occurs as a variant of the horn-blowing expressions. In an Internet discussion about how to refer politely to a 'fart', the questioner was told that 'the answer, my friend, is blowing in the wind.'

Blow one's nose

H. Montgomery Hyde, in *A History of Pornography*, remarks that 'the great English Greek scholar Dr Gilbert Murray always insisted upon translating the verb meaning "to break wind" as "to blow one's nose."' Murray, who was actually born in Sydney, Australia, had strict views about what he considered to be obscenity. 'Blowing one's nose' was presumably as close as he allowed himself to come to 'blowing off'.

Blue streak

The phrases 'farted a blue streak' and 'pooted a blue streak' were quoted by American respondents to a questionnaire about how they described 'breaking wind from the bowels'. In American English, 'to talk a blue streak' is to talk very quickly, the allusion probably being to a flash of lightning. 'Blue' is also associated with intestinal gas because of 'blue angel' (see *Methane*).

In Britain 'Blue Streak' was at one time associated with a military weapon, abandoned in 1960 because of its high cost and the fact that it could only be fired from a fixed launching-pad. Farts do not as yet seem to have been used as military weapons, though it could be argued that 'fartillery' would have distinct advantages. Farts cost nothing at all and are fired from highly mobile launching-pads. Perhaps this idea lies behind the slang expression 'firing flatus', used by some speakers as a synonym for 'passing gas'.

Blurting

An Australian informant reports that this is his family word for breaking wind. As it happens, the dictionaries state that 'blurt' was formed by combining a word like 'blow' or 'blast' with 'spurt' or 'squirt', so it seems especially apt to use it in a flatulent context. In early use, to blurt at someone was to make a pooh-poohing noise of contempt.

Bombus

Latin *bombus* 'boom' is used technically to describe both a humming noise in the ears and 'the sonorous movement of flatus in the intestines', the kind of movement that often precedes an escape of gas. In a Latin-English glossary of the mid-sixteenth century, Richard Huloet equates 'bombus' more directly with fart words such as 'crack'.

Bonsai

'4 July 1985 Oh! the rubbish that comes thro' the post! Today there is a letter about a Japanese Bonsai tree alleging that it *farts* and imagining anyone cares!'

Russell Davies (ed.), *The Kenneth Williams Diaries*

Borborygmus

A technical term for the gurgling or rumbling noise in the intestines that precedes an escape of gas, described by some humorists as 'your stomach talking to you'. 'Intonation' seems to have been used in the past to describe the same phenomenon. It takes a poet, however, to come up with a far more interesting word. Ogden Nash, remarking that he feels 'as unfit as a fiddle', adds: 'And it is the result of a certain turbulence of the mind and a certain burbulence in the middle.'

Bottom burp

A British schoolboy euphemism for a breaking of wind, made more widely known by its use in the television series *The Young Ones*. 'Burp' alone is also sometimes used. An American correspondent reports hearing a child say, 'My fanny burped,' after passing wind. This would be an impossible thing to say in Britain, where a woman's 'fanny' is at the front rather than the back. Rather similar to 'bottom burp' is 'botty banger'.

Bounce

One of the early meanings of this verb was 'make a loud noise'. Richard Huloet's Latin-English glossary, published in the mid-sixteenth century, says that it could also mean a loud escape of anal wind. Modern use of the word suggests 'forcible ejection' in a different way, as when a night-club bouncer compels someone to leave the premises.

Bowel howl

An inventive 'fart' euphemism which deserves wider recognition because of its satisfying rhyme. It contrasts nicely with the 'silent but violent' type of emission.

Brain fart

Royal Navy slang for a mental aberration. It is also known as a 'mind fart'.

Brave-farted men

This pleasant little pun on 'brave-hearted men' occurs in Urquhart's translation of Rabelais, published in 1694. 'Half-hearted' lends itself to similar treatment.

Break company

An interesting 'fart' synonym reported by an American student. The allusion could be both to gas which is parting company from its human container and the effect that a bad smell has on a group of people, causing them to disperse.

Break off

A former English dialectal form of 'break wind'. 'Fart off' and 'crack off' are other dialectal forms. 'Let off', based on the idea of letting off a firework, is also well established.

Break wind

This is the commonest euphemism for 'fart' in modern Britain, though it is less familiar in other English-speaking countries.

Several American correspondents, for example, have said that the expression was made known to them only 'by literature', though there is evidence that it is used colloquially in various parts of the United States. A Canadian informant says that, to his knowledge, the phrase would only be used 'self-consciously'. Some support for this view is found in the fact that nothing untoward was seen in naming a modern American garment a 'wind-breaker', even though a fart itself can be described by such a term. In former times 'wind-breaker' would instead have been used of something with carminative properties, helping to prevent the build up of flatus.

'Break wind' has been used in its farting sense since at least the sixteenth century, by which time 'wind' was also established in its 'flatus' sense. It is clear that 'break wind' was used originally of both farting and belching, and perhaps especially of the latter. There was formerly a verb 'brake', which meant to spew or vomit. It is possible, therefore, that 'brake wind' was reinterpreted as 'break wind'. When Bailey compiled his *Universal Etymological English Dictionary* in the eighteenth century he defined 'fart' as 'to break wind backwards'. To 'belch' was to 'break wind upwards'.

Breath test

Dr Michael Levitt, of Minneapolis, has developed a breath-alyser test which can check for incipient flatulence. If there is excess hydrogen in a patient's breath, it probably indicates excess gas elsewhere. Reporting on this in *Discover Magazine*, Jeffrey Kluger remarked that 'if Levitt is checking his patients' breath for flatulence, I wouldn't even ask how he'd propose to conduct dental work.'

Breeze

To 'breeze' is an alternative slang form of 'break wind', while a 'breezer', according to G.A. Wilkes, in A *Dictionary of Australian Colloquialisms*, is juvenile Australian slang for a fart.

The latter expression clearly has wider currency: Dr Terrence Keough reports that when he was a schoolboy in Canada, a rhyme that was passed on from one generation of Latin students to the next was:

> Julius Caesar blew a breezer on the coast of France,
> His brother tried to do the same and did it in his pants.

In *The Unexpurgated Code*, J.P. Donleavy remarks that farts 'are, in circles of the most haughty particularity, always referred to as personal breezes'. There was a seventeenth-century saying 'to have a breeze in one's breech', but surprisingly, this had nothing to do with breaking wind. It meant to be perturbed by something.

Brewer's fart

To 'let a brewer's fart', in eighteenth- and nineteenth-century slang, meant to befoul oneself. 'Brewer's fizzle', by contrast, was used to refer to beer. In modern British slang a 'brew' is sometimes used to refer to a smelly exhalation.

PLUS JE BOIS MIEUX JE CHANTE

Brompton

An English place name (examples in several counties) given a new meaning by Douglas Adams and John Lloyd in *The Meaning of Liff*. 'A brompton is that which is said to have been committed when you are convinced you are about to blow off with a resounding trumpeting noise in a public place and all that actually slips out is a tiny "pfpt".'

Bronx cheer

See *Raspberry*.

Bubbles

'Making bubbles' is a mild euphemism for breaking wind while immersed in water. This activity seems to fascinate a lot of people, perhaps because it allows them to see their own farts, which normally remain invisible. Philip Roth throws new light on such phenomena when he writes, in *Portnoy's Complaint*: 'When I fart in the bathtub, she kneels naked on the tile floor, leans all the way over, and kisses the bubbles.'

A joke reported from Missouri runs: 'You know what a hillbilly bubblebath is?' 'No.' 'Eat a can of beans before getting into the bath and you'll find out.' This idea is expanded at a web site which offers for sale a Redneck Bubble Bath,

consisting of 'natural, organic bubbles, homemade of course'. There is a spoof explanation of how the cleansing properties of bubbles created in the bath by two young lads from southern Mississippi were discovered accidentally 'around 1830'. 'The gas from inside the bubbles literally popped the dirt away.' Unfortunately an unpleasant smell also arose when the bubbles popped, but that problem has been solved with the help of another new product – BUTTfume (dreamed up by the same joker). This manages to change the odour of anal gas 'into a pleasant, natural, sweet-smelling whiff-of-excitement'. Potential buyers of the product are advised to spray it between their butt-cheeks and combine it with a natural gas emission in order to perfume a room.

Buck snort

Also buck snorter. Derived from the practice of a hunter who breaks wind loudly, then asks his companions: 'Did you hear that buck snort?' See also *Cuckoo Song*.

Bum

There is disagreement amongst philologists as to whether this mainly British slang word for the buttocks is derived from 'bottom', or from the booming sound of discharged gas (or excrement). Ernest Weekley maintains in his *Etymological Dictionary of Modern English* that 'bum' is related to a Dutch dialect word *boem*, itself related to *bodem* 'bottom'. He points out that Pepys used 'bummery' for the naval word 'bottomry', and that the contemporary French translation of the seventeenth-century 'bumbailiff' was *pousse-cul*, where *cul* means 'arse'.

Those in favour of the bum = boom theory point out that 'bottom' was not used in English in its 'buttocks' sense until long after 'bum' had established itself. They point to Italian, where 'bum' and 'boom' are apparently the same word. It might help their case if 'boom' had at some stage been used as a synonym for 'fart', but there is no evidence that this has ever happened. 'Boomer' has, however, been recorded as a term for a loud anal explosion. 'Paul Boomer' is also sometimes used as a personification of the anus, as in Hal J. Daniel's poem 'Whew, Ah': 'You lie there/in tight-assed panic/praying to Paul Boomer/you won't scorch/or sizzle/your squeezers.' See also *Bombus*.

Burbulence

See *Borborygmus*.

Burn bad powder

Reported as an American slang term for passing gas in a smelly way.

Burst at the broadside

Partridge's *Dictionary of Historical Slang* says that this was drinkers' slang for breaking wind from around 1670 to 1850, but 'burst' seems to have been in use much earlier as a euphemism for 'fart'. *The Oxford English Dictionary* has a quotation of 1532 which reads: 'to farte or to burste'. 'Burst' seems especially suitable in this context, since one of the earliest meanings of the verb was 'to break suddenly, snap, crack, under violent pressure, strain, or concussion. Chiefly said of things possessing considerable capacity for resistance and breaking with loud noise.' This seems to be a good description of a loud escape of anal gas bursting upon the scene.

Butt sneeze

Euphemistic for 'a fart'. 'Butt explosion' also occurs. 'Butt' is sometimes given the unnecessary adjectival form 'buttal'. Although 'butt' looks like a slang abbreviation of 'buttock', it is the older of the two terms. 'Buttock' is actually a diminutive of 'butt', in its sense of 'the thick end of something'. To 'butt in' (where one is not wanted) is a relatively modern phrase, and appears to have no connection with buttocks. Nevertheless, 'butting into a conversation' would be a useful way of referring to the impolite person who breaks wind loudly near people who are talking. See also *Perdological salutations*.

Cabbage fart

A slang expression for a particularly smelly emission, even when the eating of cabbage has not actually caused it.

Carbonated drinks

The modern method of drawing beer from a pub-cellar by means of gas pressure leads to a certain amount of the gas being transferred to the beer itself. Since all carbonated drinks encourage flatulence, beer drinkers are now even more prone to windiness than they used to be.

Carminative

'Carminative' refers to anything which prevents flatulence. The origin of the word, which has a basic meaning of 'comb, card for wool', reflects ancient medical theories. It was thought that wind was caused by 'gross humours' in the body. Carminatives were supposed to comb these out, as if they were knots in wool.

Carminative properties have at various times been claimed for aniseed, caraway, camomile, balm, sage, dittany, baldmoney, fennel, chloroform, coriander, dill, pepper and cumin. Cinnamon was also thought to prevent flatulence. In Congreve's *The Way of the World*, when a coachman calls for a 'glass of cinnamon water', Witwoud says that it must be for 'a bawd troubled with wind'. See also *Peppermints*.

Modern carminatives are more usually known as anti-flatulents. Many can be bought without prescription, but, if they are to be effective, it is necessary to know what is causing the flatulence in the first place. For instance, Beano helps to digest the sugar that is present in beans and vegetables, but would have no effect on gas caused by lactose. Those who have a lactose (dairy products) intolerance would benefit from products such as Lactaid, Lactrase and Dairy Ease.

Cheek flapper

A passing of gas which causes the halves of the buttocks to part and slap together again several times in quick succession. The use of 'cheeks' for the posterior is still considered to be slang.

Cheese

Associated with belching or breaking wind in American slang. See *Cut the cheese*.

Chesterton and Shaw

G.K. Chesterton and George Bernard Shaw were good friends, able to make fun of one another.

On one occasion Chesterton remarked that if his wife bore him a boy, he would name it Gilbert, after himself. A girl would be named Frances, after his wife. If the pregnancy proved to be nothing but wind, Chesterton added, he would call it George Bernard Shaw.

Christmas entertainment

P.H. Reaney, in *The Origins of English Surnames*, tells us that 'about 1250 Rolland le Pettour is recorded as holding land in Hemingstone (Suffolk) by serjeantry of appearing before the King every year on Christmas Day to do a jump, a whistle and a fart (*unum saltum et unum sifflum et unum bumbulum*). In another record he is called Roland le Fartere. Pettour is from the French *péter* "to break wind" and, as the word was uncommon, the meaning was forgotten. It survives in the Ipswich surname Petter and probably in Pethard, Petard.' Professor Reaney goes on to say that the modern French surnames Pétard, Peton, Petot, and probably Pétain also indicate an ancestor who was a wind-breaker, professional or otherwise.

William Camden's *Remains Concerning Britain* has another reference to the man who was farter by royal appointment. He names him as Baldwin le Pettour and says that both his name and his land derived from his official duties – '*per saltum, sufflum et pettum, sive bumbulum*, for dancing, pout-puffing, and doing that before the King of England in Christmas holy days, which the word *pet* signifieth in French.'

The idea of a man attracting royal patronage because of his ability to break wind seems extraordinary today, but it would not have surprised le Pettour's contemporaries. There is some disagreement in the two Latin accounts of his precise duties at court, but it is likely that he was a minstrel, known for his dancing, mime and ability to whistle melodiously as well as fart. It was clearly the latter skills, however, which made the strongest impression on his royal audience. William Chambers mentions in his book, *The Medieval Stage*, that farting at will 'was one of the accomplishments expected of the lower type of minstrel'. Le Pettour must have had exceptional skills, perhaps similar to those of Joseph Pujol – see *Le Pétomane*.

To quote Professor Reaney again, in the late Middle Ages, at all levels of English society, 'farting was regarded as perfectly natural and a source of considerable amusement.'

Churl's fart

The Elizabethans frequently expressed their contempt for someone by referring to a fart. Beaumont and Fletcher demonstrate one of the possibilities in *The Knight of the Burning Pestle*, where one character says to another: 'A churl's fart in your teeth, sir!'

Clanger

This occasional synonym for 'fart' was probably suggested by the phrase 'drop a clanger' – make a mistake.

Classifications

One of the writers to turn his attention successfully to the classification of gas emissions was J.P. Donleavy, in *The Unexpurgated Code*, a 'complete manual of survival and manners'. Donleavy speaks there of 'the Nert or Chirping fart', which is a ladylike 'backfired cheep, high pitched in frequency and resembling that of a small bird in song'. The Whispering or Purring fart is said to be equally suitable for ladies. Donleavy's other named farts are variously labelled the Percolating, Stammering, King, Blaster, Flash, Fake, Farewell, Foghorn, Beep, French, Swiss, Austrian, Sleeper, Requiem and Royal. Donleavy's most interesting classification is what he calls The Morse. This, he says, is met with in diplomatic circles, where it 'is greeted with some suspicion as it is often a method of communication between spies'.

Fart classification is a popular activity on the Internet. The so-called *Encyclopaedia Fartannica*, for example, describes farts which range from the Turbine, 'a high-pitched squeak', through the Grandmother, Oops, Runner's Rip, Bathtub Bubbler, to the Flamethrower. Of the last-named it is said that 'in theory, a huge blue flame shoots towards the ceiling when someone holds a match or lighter over your rear end as you fart. In reality, you burn your bum.'

Clat-fart shop

D.H. Lawrence mentions the clat-fart shop in *Sons and Lovers*:

> When the children were old enough to be left, Mrs. Morel joined the Women's Guild. It was a little club of women attached to the Co-operative Wholesale Society, which met on Monday night in the long room over the grocery shop of the Bestwood Co-op. The women were supposed to discuss the benefits to be derived from co-operation, and other social questions.
>
> The Guild was called by some hostile husbands, who found their wives getting too independent, the "clat-fart" shop – that is, the gossip-shop. It is true, from off the basis of the Guild, the women could look at their homes, at the conditions of their own lives, and find fault. So the colliers found their women had a new standard of their own, rather disconcerting.

'Clat' was used in several regional dialects to refer to 'tittle-tattle.' It was occasionally a specific reference to a woman's tongue and the clatter it supposedly made. The '-fart' of 'clat-fart' was a derisive male comment on the windiness of the female speakers.

Clearing the nether throat

A euphemistic phrase which refers to farting. In Mark Twain's 1601, Sir Walter Raleigh breaks wind in the presence of Elizabeth I and explains: 'I did it but to clear my nether throat.' The word 'nether', almost never used in modern English, means 'under, lower'. Tim Rogers resurrects it well in his article 'Rearing' to say: 'In all but the most formal of settings, I won't hesitate to let loose the nether zephyr.'

The Netherlands were so-called because they are low-lying lands. In earlier times, a reference to 'the nether world' would have meant 'hell', which was thought to lie beneath the earth. A person's 'nether end' was his backside (see *Crack*), and expressing a wish to 'rest one's nether end' would have indicated that one wanted to sit down. In more general terms, someone's 'nether parts' were his legs, and any other parts below the waist. By the eighteenth century, in coarse slang, 'the Netherlands' had come to mean someone's private parts.

Colonic microbes

The micro-organisms which break down undigested food in the human body mostly live in the colon, part of the large intestine. As they feed they generate their own waste products, mostly in gaseous form. This becomes the flatus which humans eventually expel. The best-known colonic microbe is the E. coli. Others include the Klebsiella, Clostridium and M. smithii.

Comic Relief

The Introduction to the Comic Relief 'Fart Page' on the Internet reads: 'Welcome to the Fart Homepage, the Number One page for flatulence, farting, wind, gas, bottom burps, beefs, stewarts, rippers, air biscuits, brews, smells, cheek flappers, vapour chokes, stinkies, pocket thunder, afterburners, whiffs, and trodden-on-frogs!' There is also a reference to a 'ming', which, like 'brew', apparently means a smelly exhalation.

A 'stewart' no doubt refers to an individual of that name who is known for his flatulent prowess.

Common Scents

Bob Burton Brown, Professor of Education at the University of Florida and a former Dean of the University College, is listed in an issue of *Maledicta* as the author of *Common Scents: the first book of farts*. A thorough search of all available bibliographies has failed to reveal any trace of the work, and there is no evidence that it was ever published.

Comparisons are odorous

Studies show that two in every three of the average man's anal gas emissions have a noticeable smell. The corresponding figure for women is one in two.

Cough

There are various links between coughing and breaking wind. Sometimes a genuine fit of coughing causes the person concerned to pass gas at the same time. By long tradition, a deliberate cough can also be used in a hasty attempt to smother the sound of an involuntary escape. Eric Partridge says in *Catchwords* that 'Do you spit much with that cough?' was an enquiry heard in Canada when someone noisily broke wind in company. 'Trouser cough' is used by some speakers as a euphemism for 'fart' itself. 'Cough in your rompers' is lower-deck slang in the Royal Navy for 'fart'.

Crab

Crab is Launce's fart-prone dog in Shakespeare's play *The Two Gentlemen of Verona*. He is 'the sourest-natured dog that lives', but Launce is nevertheless ready to suffer on Crab's behalf. In Act 4 he explains to the audience:

> If I had not had more wit than he, to take a fault upon me that he did, I think verily he had been hanged for 't; sure as I live, he had suffered for 't: you shall judge. He thrusts me himself into the company of three or four gentlemanlike dogs under the duke's table: he had not been there – bless the mark! – a pissing while, but all the chamber smelt him. 'Out with the dog!' says one: 'What cur is that?' says another: 'Whip him out' says the third: 'Hang him up' says the duke. I, having been acquainted with the smell before, knew it was Crab, and goes me to the fellow that whips the dogs: 'Friend,' quoth I; 'you mean to whip the dog.' 'Ay, marry do I' quoth he. 'You do him the more wrong,' quoth I. ' 'twas I did the thing you wot of.' He makes me no more ado, but whips me out of the chamber. How many masters would do this for his servant?

John Mortimer makes use of this incident in *Rumpole and the Way Through the Woods*, when a young man concerned with animal welfare falsely pleads guilty to a crime. Rumpole tells him: 'I doubt very much whether the animals are going to be grateful to you. In fact they'll hardly notice.' He adds: 'When Crab farts at the Duke's dinner-party, Launce takes the blame for it and is whipped out of the room. Launce also sat in the stocks for puddings Crab stole and stood in the pillory for geese Crab killed. How did Crab reward him? Simply by lifting his leg and peeing against Madam Silvia's skirt. That's how much Crab appreciated Launce's extraordinary sacrifice.'

Crack
••••••

'Crack' was an early synonym for breaking wind, both as noun and verb. A fourteenth-century writer, for example, glossed 'fart' as 'a crack of the nether end'. An especially interesting use of 'crack' occurs in Philemon Holland's translation of Suetonius (1606): 'He would give folk leave to break wind downward and let it go even with a crack at the very board.' In other words, guests were told that they were free to 'let one go' at the dinner-table.

In early times there are several recorded instances where hosts of high social standing told their dinner-guests 'Feel free to pass gas at any time.' There is little doubt that the reason for the later custom of women withdrawing from the table, leaving the men with their port and cigars, was to give the men a chance to mingle the odours from their nether ends with that of the cigar smoke. Some men were unable to wait that long. Frank Harris, in My Life, relates that Lady Marriott was once 'compelled to leave her own table, at which she was entertaining Sir Robert Fowler, then the Lord Mayor of London, because of the suffocating and nauseating odours there'. Sir Robert was notorious for his smelly emissions (see also Parliamentary gas). J.P. Donleavy hints at the possible reason for this in The Unexpurgated Code when he says that 'from a full fed gentleman of long term epicurean indulgence, you could be gassed stupid and reeling before you get as far as the withdrawing room to join the fortunately absent ladies.'

'Crack' is reportedly still in use in its breaking wind sense in some American states, both as noun and verb. 'Crack a rat' also occurs. A particular type of fart, or rapid series of explosions, can also be referred to as a 'fire-cracker'.

Crank

'To crank' was reported as a synonym for 'fart' by an American student, early in 1997. Its use was possibly suggested by the sound of an engine being cranked.

Crepitate

This obsolete synonym for the verb 'fart' (together with 'crepitation' as a noun) might usefully be revived for refined conversations. Technically, perhaps, it should be reserved for the crackling noise occasionally heard from a rear end, since it is based on Latin *crepare*, 'crackle, creak'. The same word gave us 'decrepit', which was originally applied to a person whose joints creaked because of his great age. Crepitate was in occasional literary use in the seventeenth century, but was never a colloquial term. It is unlikely that the Elizabethans ever asked one another 'Who crepitated?'

Crepitus ventris

A Latin phrase literally meaning 'rattling noise of the stomach', but it has been used to describe 'the noisy rejection downwards of gas from the stomach and bowels', as the editors of *The Oxford English Dictionary* chose to phrase it rather than refer more directly to a noisy fart. *Flatus ventris*, by contrast, was reserved for 'a breaking wind without noise'.

Crowp

A variant of 'croup', used in English dialect of the nineteenth century. The basic meaning was 'to grunt or grumble', but a 'crowping' was defined in the *Whitby Glossary* (1855) as 'that subdued croaking heard in the bowels from flatulence'.

Cushion creeper

An escape muffled by a chair or sofa. It is also known as a cushion duster. The noise of a fart can certainly be disguised in this way, but if it is done too often the odour is likely to linger in the material. There is another kind of emission called a 'carpet creeper', perpetrated by someone who is sitting on the floor.

Cut the cheese

Keys to Crookdom, by G.C. Henderson, published in New York in 1924, mentions that 'cheesy' in the criminal slang of the time referred to anything that had a 'very bad odour'. A 'cheeser' was at one time an eructation, but is now more strongly associated with breaking wind because of 'cut the cheese'. This expression is mentioned in most American slang dictionaries as a euphemism for the verb 'fart', though there is disagreement about how widely the phrase is actually used. Some experts say that it is native to Indiana. It has also been reported as an Australian slang expression, with the occasional variant 'squeeze the cheese' for the verb, and 'burnt cheese' for the noun.

Bill King, who learned of 'cut the cheese' while living in New York but did not take it into his own vocabulary, says that 'a co-worker/subordinate who had gone to prep school at Millbrook used to reveal his social superiority by saying "Who cut the Brie?".' One might imagine an Englishman asking 'Who cut the Cheddar?' but 'cut the cheese' does not occur in Britain and the allusion would probably not be understood.

'Cut the cheese' presumably accounts for the reference in Budd Schulberg's novel *Waterfront* to a 'cheese-eater': 'You don't think we could afford to be boxed out of a deal like this on account of one lousy little cheese-eater, that Doyle bum, who goes round agitatin' and squealin' to that friggin' Crime Commission?'

As an alternative to 'cutting the cheese', some American speakers use 'cut' as a variant of 'lay' or 'let' and refer to 'cutting' or 'cutting a fart'. They might also speak of 'cutting one' or 'cutting one loose'. A contribution to an Internet forum, for example, said: 'She's a great dog, but she can sure empty a room in a hurry if you know what I mean. I realize that most dogs will occasionally cut loose with a smelly one, but our dog does it with regularity. About 1–2 days a week she goes into major gas mode. She will regularly pass gas for several hours at a whack, leaving one to wonder if there is an endless reservoir.'

The association of 'cutting' with playing-cards no doubt led to 'cut the deck', another euphemism reported by American students in 1997. 'Cut a melon' has also been recorded, perhaps with reference to a squishy sound, though Khushwant Singh, in *Delhi, a Novel*, writes: 'My photographer friend demonstrated the Trumpet [a loud fart] by consuming a succulent watermelon on an empty stomach. An hour later he was airborne like a jet plane.' 'Cut the mustard' refers instead to breaking wind in an especially smelly way.

Daoism

A 1996 BBC television programme about the first Chinese emperor included comments on Daoism. The commentator remarked that Chinese Daoists believe that everyone is allotted a certain amount of air at birth which it is important to conserve. Belching and farting are considered to shorten one's life. Daoists therefore carefully control their diet, avoiding foods which lead to flatulence.

D-Generation, The

This is an Australian comedy show, put together by a group of university students, which contains much fart-based humour. In a typical sketch a glamorous woman was advertising a new perfume called Flatulence. There was much sniffing, with comments like 'It's me – no, it's you – no, it's definitely me.'

Dial a traf

This is 'laid a fart' with the key-words spelled backwards. Professor Susan Whitebook reports hearing the expression used when she was a student at Yale University, as in, 'Someone's dialled a traf.' 'Traf' is itself sometimes used for the verb 'fart' according to an Australian correspondent. A backward spelling seems rather appropriate for what might be called a backward phenomenon.

Did you get any on you?

Jack Chambers reports from Canada that this question is likely to be asked when a boy passes gas noisily amongst a group of his male friends.

Diet control

Some foods are likely to produce more intestinal gas than others, though a particular food which has this effect on one person may not affect another. Those who feel that they suffer from excess flatulence, however, should pay particular attention to the following items: apples, apricots, beans, bran, broccoli, Brussels sprouts, cabbage, carrots, cauliflower, nuts, onions, peaches, pears, popcorn, prunes and raisins. They should then try to reduce their intake of the items which trial and error prove to be affecting them most directly.

Dairy products should be avoided by people who are allergic to lactose, the natural sugar which is present in milk. This applies especially to those who have an African or Asian background, since they will tend to have low levels of lactase, the enzyme that digests lactose. Lactose intolerance can easily be diagnosed by a breath or blood test, but if there is doubt about what is causing the flatulence, sufferers should record what they eat and drink and make a note of the subsequent effects.

In general terms, everyone should expect a high roughage diet to produce extra flatulence, especially if the amount of roughage is increased rapidly. Since high fibre diets are now far more popular than they once were, it is likely that people are now expelling more gas than at any previous moment in history. The rise of the 'flatus factor', as the phenomenon is known, is also influenced by non-dietary considerations. People now live longer, and the elderly are more likely to suffer from constipation and take less exercise. Both of these can increase flatulence.

Disciplinary matters

A link between farting and discipline occurs in French, where a strict disciplinarian is known as a *péte-sec*, literally a 'dry fart'. In more general terms, the sound of someone breaking wind during a covert military or criminal operation might reveal the presence of someone who wishes to remain undetected. This accounts for the comment in Morris West's novel *Proteus*: 'I've told them that I'll kill the first son-of-a-bitch who even breaks wind without an order.'

The point about inadvertently revealing someone's presence was also made by an article in the *New York Daily News*, October 1995. A man described as a 'career criminal' had been apprehended in the middle of a burglary at a Fire Island home. The residents had risen to check out noises in the house but found no one. They were about to return to bed when they heard the sound of a muffled fart. Richard Magpiong, 56, was discovered hiding in a closet and was detained until the police arrived.

Disguising an embarrassing noise

Coughing or clearing the throat loudly are the usual ways of trying to disguise the sound of a fart, but other methods may be used. There was a web site available in 1997 which made some suggestions about 'ways of farting in public without being noticed', but most of the ideas put forward, it must be said, were impractical. It is not always convenient, for instance, to 'do it under water and hope that you don't kill too many fish'. An American schoolboy's suggestion that, if about to pass gas in the classroom you should hastily use the pencil sharpener, was slightly more to the point, as one might say, but that is hardly something one can do too often. Decidedly ingenious was Paul A. Caruana's suggestion that someone who passes gas frequently should 'learn the art of anal ventriloquism'. This is perhaps easier than it sounds, since it is often difficult, in a room where several people are gathered, to pinpoint the source of a fart.

Attempts to disguise the noise of a fart have been practised for centuries. A lady who once broke wind at the dinner-table in the presence of the Bishop of Orleans hastily scraped the floor with her feet and chair. The bishop told her kindly: 'Do not trouble to find a rhyme, Madam.'

Donor

Professor Terry Bolin and Rosemary Stanton, the Australian authors of *Wind Breaks*, state that 'donor' refers to 'one who emits flatus, either overtly or surreptitiously'. This is presumably on the analogy of a blood donor, who gives blood for the benefit of others. The 'donation' of intestinal gas is for the benefit of anyone who happens to be near. Khushwant Singh makes use of the same word in *Delhi, a Novel* when he says of 'the noiseless stinkbomb' kind of emission: 'The donor can assume a "not I" look on his face or hold his nostrils and turn towards someone else with an accusing look.' Singh goes on to refer to someone who passes gas as a 'benefactor': 'if you have let off a stinking *gupta daan*, let others guess the identity of the benefactor.'

Doorknob

See *Touch bone and whistle*.

Dramatic flatulence

Escanaba in da Moonlight, a stage play by Jeff Daniels, was said to 'break new theatrical ground – to say nothing of wind', when it was first performed in 1955. In Act Two a group of hunters are together in a cabin. When a supernatural white light causes one of them to go into a trance, his beer-soaked friends decide that only the flatulent efforts of his friend Jimmer can bring him out of it. A review in the *Detroit News* said that the resulting scene eclipsed even the campfire sequence in *Blazing Saddles*.

Drop a bomb

This is a euphemism for 'fart' used by British schoolchildren, who are also likely to talk about 'dropping one' and 'dropping a few'. 'Drop the bomb' was also included in a list of 'fart' synonyms prepared by American students early in 1997. The same basic idea is in the minds of those speakers who use 'explode' for 'break wind', or refer to the fart itself as an 'explosion'. 'Bang' is also used, both as noun and verb, while some flatulators talk of 'having the bangs'. Finally, there are those for whom passing gas is simply 'making a rude noise', and an attack of flatulence is being 'noisy'.

Drop one's guts

An expression used by some Australians with reference to flatulence. In this instance 'fart' might be described as a euphemism for 'drop one's guts' rather than the other way round.

Drop one's handbag

This is mentioned in *Jackspeak*, Rick Jolley's dictionary of naval slang, as a milder version of 'drop one's guts'.

Dutch oven

This is created when someone breaks wind when in bed with someone else, then buries his partner's head beneath the sheets in order to enforce an appreciation of the smell. The name is said to refer to the cooking method which uses steam in an enclosed container. Comedy sketches based on the Dutch oven have been much employed on Australian television in recent years by the *The D-Generation* team.

Normally, if one happens to be in bed with someone else when one farts, it should not be assumed that the other person will wish to savour the smell. By an unwritten rule, in fact, a flatulator sharing a bed is expected to face his partner so that he backfires in the other direction. It is also thought to be polite for the breaker of wind to lift the bedclothes behind him to allow the smell to escape.

Most people fart while they are still in bed, soon after waking. It is a way of greeting the new day, as it were. These morning emissions can sometimes be especially loud, frightening the dog or cat who sleeps on the bed-covers and waking a still-sleeping partner. The notion that human gas emissions can frighten domestic animals may seem far-fetched, but Gabriel García Márquez, in *Of Love and Other Demons*, says of Bernarda Cabrera: 'her siren's body became bloated and coppery as a three-day-old corpse and she broke wind in pestilential explosions that startled the mastiffs.'

Dysflatulence

This refers to the inability to break wind in a normal way, a physical condition which can lead to great pain for the person concerned. It is likely to affect a patient who has undergone certain types of surgery. Ardith K. Blackwell, writing in the

American Journal of Nursing, seriously recommended some years ago that such patients should stand, or be stood, on their heads. Her theory was that because gas rises, this would help it to escape. She added that nurses often suggested that patients should walk about. This could indeed provide temporary relief for the patients, but it was sometimes proposed for the nurses' own benefit. It got the patients out of hearing and smell range.

A correspondent who underwent a radical prostatectomy some years ago reports that the nurses who attended him were more sympathetic. 'I was being cajoled by the pretty young nurses to "pass gas", as they delicately put it. The day I finally ripped off an explosion that would have pleased M. Pujol (see *Le Pétomane*) they clapped their little hands in delight.'

Educated farting

The *Winnipeg Free Press* once reported that educated people break wind less often than those without college degrees. The extraordinary comment was based on a telephone survey commissioned by Block Drug Company, makers of Phazyme, a simethicone antiflatulent. Perhaps those with degrees are in a higher financial bracket and able to be fussy about what they eat. It is hard to believe that intestinal gas is a respecter in itself of academic qualifications.

Egyptian envoy

Herodotus tells the story of a flatulation which played its part in Egyptian history. It concerns Apries, King of Egypt, who reigned for twenty years in the sixth century BC. In the Old Testament he is referred to as Hophra, and Jeremiah speaks of him as 'Much-noise-but-he-lets-the-chance-slip-by'.

This Apries sent an envoy to Amasis, one of his army officers. By way of reply, Amasis, on horseback, raised his buttocks and broke wind, telling the envoy to 'catch that and deliver it to your royal master.' Apries was unable to avenge this terrible insult. Soon afterwards he was assassinated by the followers of Amasis, who succeeded him as king.

Elevators

It is considered to be unsportsmanlike to break wind in an elevator. See *Flatulate*, *Matters of Etiquette*, *Painting the Elevator*.

There is a story about a distinguished-looking English gentleman who silently breaks wind in an elevator. The elevator boy is so overcome by the foul odour that he says without thinking: 'Excuse me sir, have you just farted?' The Englishman is outraged. 'FARTED! Have I just FARTED? Of course I have, you silly bugger. Do you think I smell like this all the time?'

Embarrassing moments

Countless people have no doubt been embarrassed when they have broken wind at an inopportune moment. As Robert Fusco, M.D., says in an Internet article: 'Gas in itself is not dangerous; its main consequence is usually embarrassment and social isolation for the person who can't turn it off. Usually at the most inopportune moment, our body pulls a fast one, emitting offensive sounds or odours.'

Dr Fusco also makes the point that 'when the human being was designed millions of years ago, there were few confining walls, so gas wasn't the social problem that it can be today.'

Some people are more embarrassed by breaking wind than others. John Aubrey records in his *Brief Lives* the case of Edward de Vere, Earl of Oxford, who was unlucky enough to break wind loudly as he was 'making of his low obeisance' before Elizabeth I. He would have been facing her as he bowed, but there were no doubt many courtiers behind him who laughed at his discomfiture. Aubrey says that de Vere himself 'was so abashed and ashamed' that he immediately left England and travelled abroad for seven years. On his return he presented himself to the Queen, who welcomed him home and then remarked: 'Ah, yes, I had forgotten the fart.'

J.P. Donleavy, in *The Unexpurgated Code*, mentions some situations where an involuntary anal explosion is especially embarrassing. He includes: 'during lectures on art, largo passages in symphonies, high points in religious ceremony, or when another is spiritually transported in the rapturous delirium of orgasm'. Disturbing the silent atmosphere of a reference library with a loud trumpeting can also attract unwanted attention.

Donleavy's comment about breaking wind during a religious ceremony is supported by a story that appeared in *The Big Issue*. According to the article, an Italian priest was attacked by his congregation after letting fly in the pulpit. Father Eusebio Dodona of Naples, was, ironically, delivering a sermon on air pollution when the accident happened. 'He appeared to stiffen as if he had been poked with a stick,' recalled one worshipper, 'and then there was a thunderous roar.' The flatulent father endeavoured to continue his address, but his words were drowned out as the congregation began chanting 'Windy' over and over again. Father Dodona has since left the priesthood and set up a co-operative for melon farmers.

Erasmus

Erasmus of Rotterdam (1465–1536), one of the most eminent classical scholars of his day, believed that the rules of correct social behaviour should be instilled at an early age. His work *On Civility in Children* gives advice along the lines of: 'To lick greasy fingers or to wipe them on your coat is impolite. It is better to use the table cloth or the serviette.' He also says that: 'You should not offer your handkerchief to anyone unless it has been freshly washed. Nor is it seemly, after wiping your nose, to spread out your handkerchief and peer into it as if pearl and rubies might have fallen out of your head.'

Erasmus then turns his attention to the passing of gas. He advises his young readers that they could 'retain wind by compressing the belly'. No doubt he was speaking from personal experience, but in that case he should have known that deliberately retaining one's wind is seldom a good idea. He also makes the curious observation: 'Do not move back and forth on your chair. Whoever does that gives the impression of constantly breaking or trying to break wind.'

Escape

'Escape' was formerly used for 'fart', though its frequency of use in ordinary conversation caused it to be reduced to 'scape'. See more at *Scape*.

Excuse me!

Henry Miller complains in *Tropic of Cancer* about an Indian for whom he works temporarily: 'Sometimes when I'm drinking a cup of pale tea in which he has dropped a rose leaf he comes alongside of me and lets a loud fart, right in my face. He never says "Excuse me!" The word must be missing from his Gujarati dictionary.'

Polite convention certainly demands that someone who breaks wind in another's presence should excuse himself, but in an all-male group the flatulator may tend to celebrate his achievement rather than express his regret for it. See *Perdological salutations*. The Henson family reports that their young son, taught to say 'pardon' when he broke wind, now refers to a fart itself as a 'pardon'.

Exhalation

A euphemism for 'fart', sometimes preceded by a qualifying word such as rectal, anal or sphincteral.

Exhortations

Khushwant Singh, in *Delhi, a Novel*, writes that exhortations to the fart are found in English literature. He cites:

> Men of letters, 'ere we part
> Tell me why you never fart?
> Never fart? Dear Miss Bright,
> I do not need to fart, I write.

Singh is parodying Byron:

> Maid of Athens, ere we part,
> Give, oh give me back my heart!
> Or, since that has left my breast,
> Keep it now, and take the rest!

Expel
......

'Expel' is used by some speakers with reference to passing gas, especially in objective statements about farting as a human activity. Breaking wind is said to be 'expelling air, expelling flatus, expelling gas' or simply 'expelling'. The word implies a more positive action than merely 'passing gas'. The person who 'expels' it makes it clear that he is forcibly getting rid of something that is unwanted.

Expressing one's feelings
....

A character in J.P. Donleavy's *The Beastly Beatitudes of Balthazar B* remarks: 'I'm as usual conducting a most well run

lift. Giving smart salutes to those passengers deserving it. And slipping out a morsel of a fart at others meeting with my displeasure.' This is a literal interpretation of the seventeenth-century saying 'I fart at thee.' See also *Oppedere*.

Exterminal gas

Professor Bob Burton Brown reports that this 'quasi-technical term was coined by my youngest son to describe particularly smelly expulsions of intestinal gas – the kind that could exterminate you.'

Family entertainment

Dr Daniel Long, who lectures in Japan, writes: 'I am from Tennessee, where farting was a form of family entertainment until the advent of radio and television broadcasts. We certainly enjoyed it when I was in elementary school. It was "cutting the cheese" or "killing the Easter bunny" (don't know where that came from).' See also *Gunshots*.

Famous fart

One of the best-known passages in modern literature about breaking wind occurs in J. D. Salinger's *The Catcher in the Rye*. It is famous not only because the novel has sold millions of copies: the incident described strikes a chord with anyone who was once at school. It is difficult to believe that there is a school anywhere which has not in its time known a similar occasion.

The passage runs:

> This guy sitting in the row in front of me, Edgar Marsalla, laid this terrific fart. It was a very crude thing to do, in chapel and all, but it was also quite amusing. Old Marsalla. He damn near blew the roof off. Hardly anybody laughed out loud, and old Ossenburger made out like he didn't even hear it, but old Thurmer, the headmaster, was sitting right next to him on the rostrum and all, and you could tell he heard it. Boy, was he sore.

Farsi

· · · · ·

A Farsi-speaking correspondent reports that 'break wind' in that language is *guzidan*, which sounds like *goosedan*. The word

can also be used metaphorically. When an important person makes a mistake, for instance, it might be said that he *guzeed*. Another term is *badesh dar raft*, where *bad* is 'air' or 'gas' and *dar raft* means 'to go out'.

'Fart'
······

Philologists assume, from the fact that words like 'verten, farten, farton' and the like are recorded in Middle English, and the words *ferzan, verzen, vurzen, varzen, farzen* occur in other Germanic languages, that there was an Old English verb *feortan*, the ancestor of our word 'fart'. The Old English word is normally written as **feortan* in the dictionaries, the * indicating that it is a postulated form; no actual example is recorded in surviving Old English texts. 'Fart' ultimately belongs to the Indo-Germanic group of languages. It is distantly related to Latin *pedere* and Greek *perdein* 'to fart'.

The primary meaning of the verb 'fart' is 'break wind', with the noun simply meaning 'a breaking of wind'. Secondary meanings of the noun developed from the idea of a fart being something worthless or contemptible. In the seventeenth century a man might say that he 'cared not a fart' for something or someone. This usage seems to have survived in some quarters, since a recent novel by Frank McCourt, *Angela's Ashes*, has: 'English soldiers were sent home but they didn't give a fiddler's fart about the Irish soldiers, whether they lived or died.' In modern times references to people as 'old farts' have also become relatively frequent.

The meaning of the verb has also been extended. Because farting is considered to be a non-productive activity, we get references to 'farting about', or 'farting around'. In *Anglo-Saxon Attitudes*, Angus Wilson refers to 'some farting nonsense', where 'farting' could be glossed as 'worthless'. These expressions could be described as slang, but 'fart' itself was formerly a normal English word. *The Oxford Thesaurus* therefore has no justification for describing it as 'taboo slang', it is simply a word like 'lavatory' for which a euphemism is normally employed.

The artificial restrictions on the use of 'fart' in polite conversation appear to have begun in the sixteenth century. At the end of the 20th century it is probably true to say that the majority of people in English-speaking countries still avoid using it in mixed company. The most frequently used euphemistic synonyms are pass gas, break wind, fizzle, poop, poot, toot and trump.

There are signs that this situation is changing. Expressions such as 'arty-farty', 'fart around' and 'old fart' are now regularly heard in radio and television programmes. 'Fart' itself, in its primary meaning of break wind, is beginning to be used in quality newspapers. Perhaps an appreciation of the humour associated with flatulence will also return if 'fart' once again becomes an acceptable word that can be used in normal conversation. [See also the *Introduction* for comments by Peter Furze about the taboo status of this word.]

Fart about, to

This twentieth-century expression, meaning 'to fool about, to waste time', was originally dialectal. The *English Dialect Dictionary* (1900) has: 'thoo's allus farten aboot, thoo's warse ner a hen wi' egg.' In modern times a workman might be told to stop farting about if there was something that needed to be done as a matter of urgency. The speaker would usually be another man.

'Fart around' is a variant of this expression, as when Lisa Alther writes in *Kinflicks*: 'They wanted to fart around in the garden all day and come in and find that the womenfolk had hot meals waiting for them.' When Henry Miller, in *Tropic of Cancer*, says that 'the British, in their usual fumbling farting way, had kept us on pins and needles,' he means that British officials had, in his view, been farting around.

Another phrasal verb based on 'fart' is 'fart along', to do something very slowly, without conviction. Examples of usage would be: 'He just farts along writing his thesis.' 'That car in front of us holding up traffic is just farting along.'

Fart-arse

To 'fart-arse about' is a stronger version of to 'fart about'. 'Fart-arsed' is also used in British slang of a clumsy person, as in a 'fart-arsed mechanic'.

Fartatious

Used of a person who feels inclined to break wind, rather as a person who is flirtatious is in the mood to be coquettish.

Fart box

This is recorded in some reference works as British slang for the buttocks, but the expression is little used.

Fart catcher

A term humorously applied to a footman in former times. The footman normally walked along the street immediately behind his master or mistress and was well placed to 'catch' a windy escape.

Fartee

There are many pairs of words in English where the suffix -ee indicates a passive relationship to an agent noun ending in -er. Examples include interviewee, interviewer; trainee, trainer; employee, employer; examinee, examiner, and so on. It is therefore perhaps surprising that 'fartee' is not in general use as the person who suffers the consequences of someone else's fart. The phrase 'passive farting' has been coined to describe the situation where a fartee is unwillingly exposed to the odours of a farter, especially in a confined space such as an elevator or a small office. No doubt the day will come when an employee/fartee seeks legal compensation for the effects of passive farting.

Farters Anonymous

'An alcoholic promising not to drink again is roughly like anyone promising never to fart again.'

Norman Rush, *Mating*

Fart frankincense, to

In 1710 the *British Apollo* magazine asked: 'What is meant when we say "a man farts frankincense"?' The comment implies that the saying had recently come into general use, though it is not recorded elsewhere. It is not known whether any answer was given to the question at the time, but it appears to be the sort of thing that is said about someone who always comes out on top, no matter what he does. A modern equivalent might be: 'If he fell into a cesspit he'd still come up smelling of roses.'

Farticane

A humorous neologism based on 'hurricane', referring to a powerful blowing of wind.

Farting clapper

A slang reference to the 'rump' in British slang of the late nineteenth and early twentieth centuries.

Farting club

An article in the *San Francisco Examiner* (13 August, 1977) by Donald Zochert says that '18th century London had a club devoted to the public practice of this private art,' namely farting. It has not, unfortunately, been possible to obtain further details of this intriguing society, but its motto deserves to live on: 'Any man can make a noise. Not every man can add a flavour.'

Farting Fanny

A name given by British soldiers in World War One to a German long-range gun. It was later replaced by the name used by the Germans themselves, Big Bertha, an allusion to Bertha Krupp. The steel and engineering works of the Krupp family firm had provided Germany with its armament.

Farting shot

This refers to farting as one leaves the room, a perdological parting shot which enables one to have – if not the last word – the last comment.

Farting spell

A British slang reference to 'a short space of time'. To 'have a farting spell', however, can mean to 'lose control, lose one's temper'.

Fartkin

In his *Dictionary of Historical Slang*, Eric Partridge says that 'fartkin' and 'fartick' were used as colloquial 'diminutives of fart' in the nineteenth century. There are no examples of either term in *The Oxford English Dictionary*.

Fart language

'He laughed inordinately when I was getting into bed and slightly farted and he said Is that the way you greet me? I replied quick as a flash That's the only language you understand. Neither of us could figure out why we thought this was funny, but we both did.'

Norman Rush, *Mating*

Fartleberries

A word that was brought to the attention of a wider public when used as the name of a pop group. It normally refers to the dried pieces of excrement which cling to the anal hair of farmyard animals, or of those human beings who do not regularly take a shower.

Fartlek

This Swedish word was imported into English in the 1950s by athletes specializing in middle- and long-distance running. *Fart* in this instance means 'speed', *lek* is 'play'. Using the fartlek system of training, the athlete runs across country mixing spells of fast running with spells of jogging. Farting in the normal sense does not come into it, although some runners say that an occasional backfire gives them a little extra propulsion.

Fart limericks

In accordance with Peter Furze's wishes, fart limericks – almost invariably coarse in tone – are omitted from the main body of *Tailwinds*. Readers who are not overly offended by coarse language may if they wish read some examples of the genre, including the classic 'There was a young man from Sparta', in *Appendix 2* of this book.

Fartman

A character created by the American radio presenter Howard Stern. Fartman was made known to an international audience in 1997 by the release of *Private Parts*, a movie based on Stern's book of the same name. It tells the story of Stern's rise to fame.

Fart-off

An article in *American Speech*, volume 21, by Fred Eikel, was concerned with the special slang expressions used at the 'Aggie', the Agricultural and Mechanical College of Texas. One term peculiar to the school was 'fart-off', meaning an insult. The word could also be used as a verb in the same sense, 'to fart-off someone'.

Fart Proudly

This is the title of a paperback which contains several short pieces by Benjamin Franklin, including his spoof letter to the Royal Academy of Brussels, in which he calls for scientists to investigate how to make farts smell pleasant. The editor of this collection, Carl Japinski, also imagines himself having a conversation with Franklin about life in modern America. The words 'fart proudly' are attributed to Franklin at the end of this imaginary conversation. Most Americans, however, now seem to be convinced that Franklin really did tell his countrymen to 'fart proudly'.

Farts, the

Some people suffering from an attack of flatulence announce quite simply that they 'have the farts'.

Fart sack

This is a slang term for a sleeping-bag or bed, used by the armed services in all English-speaking countries, also by Scouts, etc. It is just possible that 'fart sack' was originally the term in expressions like 'hit the sack', 'sack time', 'sack drill', 'sack duty' – the last three referring to time a soldier spends in bed.

Farts for sale

There was a persistent rumour among English schoolboys in the late 1940s that in Germany it was possible to buy farts. It is now thought that this idea arose because of a simple misunderstanding. A few English soldiers returning home after World War Two had reported overhearing German citizens asking *Was kostet die Fahrt?* They had naïvely assumed that the enquiry was about the cost of a fart, instead of the price of a journey.

Fart the 'Star-spangled Banner'

A former American slang expression which ironically referred to being able to do anything that one was asked to do and a whole lot more. Bill King has suggested that the phrase may have referred to the stage-performances of Joseph Pujol at the end of the nineteenth century. See also *Le Pétomane.*

Farty

For some reason this word is not mentioned in *The Oxford English Dictionary, Chambers English Dictionary* or any other dictionaries that have been consulted. Beryl Bainbridge instinctively makes use of it in her novel, *Sweet William.* She writes: 'Nurse Borman had borrowed Mrs Kershaw's chicken casserole to bath the baby in. "She's a vegetarian," muttered Ann. "She stews beans in that. Farty beans." And she giggled.'

Fatal flatus

A bizarre web site page entitled 'Death by Flatulence' passed on a report said to originate with the AP wire service. It concerned a man who died in a room which had little or no ventilation and was filled with his own stale gas. According to this report 'there was no mark on the body, but an autopsy showed large amounts of methane gas in his system.' The man concerned was said to have been big, with a huge capacity for creating this gas. It was also claimed that three of the would-be rescuers who found his body became sick themselves because they inhaled the gas. Later postings to the web site went to great lengths to prove that the report was nonsensical, merely 'an urban legend', the type of story that is dreamed up by a group of men in a bar.

A Reuter report in April 1995, however, did show that flatus could, at least indirectly, be fatal to those who emitted it. A South African Airways jet carrying 300 passengers from England to South Africa had been forced to turn back and make an emergency landing because a fire alarm had been set off in the cargo hold. It was subsequently found that 72 stud pigs in the hold had been passing gas profusely. As well as triggering the alarm, their flatus had eventually caused the automatic release of a fire-suppressing gas called halon. Although there was no actual fire to put out, the halon had suffocated 15 of the pigs. They had, in effect, been killed by their own farts.

For the possibility of fart-methane being a contributing factor in the extinction of the dinosaurs, see *Global warming*.

Feminine toots
....

An unwritten social rule admits that men need to break wind but pretends that women live in a permanently fart-free zone. Tracy Catlin, for example, in an autobiographical essay made available on the Internet, entitles her piece 'Ladies Don't Fart'. What they do, she later explains, is *rosepetal* or *toot*. She compares the feminine fart situation with the well-known saying:

> Here's a little proverb that you surely ought to know:
> Horses sweat and men perspire, but ladies only glow.

Many men are embarrassed if they break wind in the presence of a woman, especially if they are in the early stages of a relationship, but the embarrassment of a woman who is the guilty party in such circumstances is usually much greater. Bernard Malamud, in *Dubin's Lives*, has a scene where a young woman and a man are alone in intimate circumstances for the first time. Malamud writes: 'When she bent to remove his socks there was a tearing noise. "What was that?" Fanny laughed wildly. "I farted." She ran with a sob into the bathroom.'

Many would say that in this instance it was the man who was at fault. There is another unwritten rule which says that if a lady does happen to break wind, a gentleman turns a deaf ear to it. He hears no evil, nor does he smell it. Even better, he quickly excuses himself as if he were the culprit. Under no circumstances does he force a lady to admit that it was she who was responsible for that unmistakable sound of escaping gas.

Fetishism

Forum discussions on the Internet make it clear that there are some men whose sexual satisfaction is enhanced if they are forcibly exposed to a partner's anal emissions. Presumably this comes into the general realm of dominance, and the need some individuals have of being humiliated.

Filters

The *Daily Telegraph* carried an item (30 November, 1996) headed 'Begone with the wind' about the invention of an anti-flatulence device called the Fartypants Filter. Tom Costello, 34, from Rugby, was quoted as saying that had the filter been invented sooner, it might have saved his marriage. Mr Costello, 'a self-confessed chronic blower-offer', was forced to create a carbon device that farters like himself could wear in their underpants when it became clear that his wife 'could not bear to be in the same street as me, let alone the same bed'. He blamed this on his love of lager and curries, 'a recipe for disaster'. His Fartypants Filter was inspired 'by the way soldiers in the First World War tried to protect themselves against mustard gas' and is claimed to be most effective. Mr Costello says: 'Wearing the filter, I have the confidence to stay in the same room at parties without constantly excusing myself.' He adds: 'I sleep with my filter in place, confident that my partner is spared my horrible gases.' Sadly, that partner is no longer his wife.

In similar vein, UltraTech Products of Houston, Texas, advertises for $29.95 a 'Flatulence Filter', otherwise known as a 'TooT TrappeR'. According to the company's announcement on the Web, this is a 'one inch thick super activated carbon air filter' concealed in a cushion. It is claimed that 'this same air filtration technology is used by the Space Shuttle program to protect the air breathed by our astronauts.' Activated carbon, it seems, was also in the gas masks worn by American soldiers during the Desert Storm war. The company makes the point that 'since the gas we produce isn't nearly so toxic as that facing soldiers, you can be assured of a pleasant atmosphere in your home, office or car.'

Another product on offer in America is Fartalis. The manufacturer's literature states that this is 'a cushionlike material designed to capture and neutralize odours at the source. It has no odour of its own and is designed to be easily placed within a bed pillow, throw pillow, or our cute Fartalis Teddy Bear. Then simply sit or roll over on it and let Fartalis stop bedroom odours at their source.' The 'cute teddy bear', together with its replaceable Fartalis Module, is priced at $15.99 and is said to be 'truly the perfect lover's gift'. The lover might need to be a skilled diplomat, however. Giving a partner a teddy bear while saying: 'sit on that and it will stop your odours at their source' requires considerable panache. PEC Fartalis operates out of Springfield, Illinois.

A Japanese company is said to have gone one better than Tom Costello's filter that has to be put in one's pants. They market underwear which is itself 'odour-eating'.

Fishy farts

A reader of the *New Scientist* magazine (1 February, 1997) asked why fish do not fart. Other correspondents assured her that they do, though the gas may be contained in a gelatinous, faecal tube and not necessarily be seen as bubbles. Alexandra Osman, in her letter of reply, commented specifically on the Sand Tiger shark, which 'has mastered the technique of farting as an extra buoyancy device'. The shark gulps in extra air on the surface and 'can then fart out the required amount of air to maintain its position at a certain depth'.

Quite what it has to do with these scientific facts is unclear, but there is a curious Texan saying: 'dry as a fish fart rolled in sand'.

Fizzle

Our ancestors made use of a number of words which defined different types of fart. A 'fizzle' was glossed by a sixteenth-century commentator as 'a close fart'. 'Close' seems to have had the sense 'quiet', since a slang dictionary of 1700 said that a fizzle was 'a little or low-sounding fart'. Tom D'Urfey commented in 1721: 'I fizzle such small puffs of wind,' while a text of 1739 has: 'now let a fizzle steal in silence forth.'

The Oxford English Dictionary is unable to find examples of 'fizzle' in its 'silent fart' sense after 1836, when B.D. Walsh made use of it in a translation of Aristophanes's *The Knights*: 'And then in court they poisoned one another with their fizzles.' However, there is ample evidence in the materials collected by the editors of the *Dictionary of American Regional English* that 'fizzle' continues to be well used in southern American states. It may also survive in some areas of Britain.

Flative

'Flative' was formerly used to mean 'producing flatulence'. An early seventeenth-century text says: 'Eat not too many of those apples, they be very flative.'

Flatology

According to Terry Bolin and Rosemary Stanton, in *Wind Breaks*, 'flatology' is 'the scientific study of intestinal gases', 'flatological' being the associated adjective. Bolin and Stanton also refer to such things as 'flatoanalysis – the determination of the nature of intestinal gases'; a 'flatogram – a chart documenting the number of times gas is passed'; 'flatogenic' – an adjective applied to 'foods likely to produce excessive gas'.

Before flatus can be studied it must be collected. One method of doing so is to insert a rubber tube into a volunteer's anus and connect it to a gas bag. A check can be carried out to see whether any gas leakage is occurring by using the system that might be employed to find a puncture in an inner tube. The volunteer is asked to sit in a bathful of water and a watch is kept for bubbles. A rather more dignified method of collecting flatus requires the donor to enter a small airtight room. Air is passed into the room at a fixed rate. Since the amount of hydrogen entering the room is known, the increased amount passing through the out-flow must have been produced by the flatulator.

Flatometer

The British biologist Dr Colin Leakey was reported in 1995 to have invented a flatometer, a device to measure flatulence. The science of assessing how much anal gas is passed is likewise known as flatometry. Dr Leakey had also produced a non-flatulent bean, which he was test-marketing in France. Journalists on both sides of the Atlantic seem to have thought it appropriate for a man called Leakey to be studying flatulence, though the name would be even more suitable for a urologist.

Flatulate

This word has not yet earned a place in the dictionaries, but together with the associated neologisms 'flatulation' and 'flatulator' it is frequently found on the web. On one home page there is even a reference to 'pyroflatulate', which presumably means to 'fart fire'. Another web source states firmly that 'men fart, women flatulate', but most users merely see 'flatulate' as a polite version of 'fart' which can be used in formal circumstances, such as those described under *Solemn considerations*.

Examples of 'flatulate' are to be found, for instance, at the web site which boasts a so-called *Dictionary of Cursing*. It has an entry: 'Flatulate, verb, to fart, poot, break wind, pass gas, frappe, lay heat.' At another site, the *Pidgin English Dictionary*, compiled by Terry D. Barhorst and Sylvia O'Dell-Barhorst, has a headword 'flatulate' which is equated with 'fart'. It says that the words for this action in Pidgin English, as spoken in Port Moresby, Papua New Guinea, are *piak* and *kapupu*. Further use of 'flatulate' occurs at the web site which lists 'Jennifer's tips on elevator etiquette'. One of these tips is: 'Please do not flatulate, or burp in the elevator, unless you have some air freshener handy!' Here one might have expected 'eructate' instead of 'burp' to match the supposed formality of 'flatulate'.

'Flatulation' appears to be used to mean both an individual breaking of wind and flatulence in general. Terry Bolin and Rosemary Stanton, in *Wind Breaks*, give it an official blessing by defining it as 'the act of expelling gas from the anus'. Some typical statements found on the Internet are: 'The flatulation from domesticated cows produces about 30 per cent of the methane on this planet'; 'fluffing the blankets after flatulation is NOT necessary'; 'common terms for flatulation: poot, blow, cut the cheese, rip/cut one, etc.'

'Flatulator' is now treated as the agent noun for a person who flatulates, as in *American Flatulators*, a video parody on *American Gladiators*. This stars Foster Solomon as Gaseous Clay, who 'floats like a butterfly and farts like a blowfish'. Solomon's wife, Kelly, has apparently stated: 'This is the role he was born to play. Trust me.' Solomon's co-star is Stella Sarcone, who plays a character called SBD. Ripper is played by Reid Mihalko, Fluff by April Hayden. The publicity material for this video perpetrates what is probably the most outrageous pun on the Web, suggesting that one of these actors might win a 'Flacademy Award.'

Flatulence

This refers to excess gas in the stomach or intestines which the body needs to expel through the anus. Or as Jeffrey Kluger expressed it in an April 1995 article in *Discover Magazine*: 'Flatulence is the means by which the body rids the colon of unwanted gases, the intestines of unwanted pressure, and crowded theatre rows of unwanted strangers.'

Every normal healthy person produces a significant amount of intestinal gas (flatus) daily; if this were not released the gases trapped within the digestive system would produce bloating and abdominal distension. The unpleasant effects of such distension may be experienced, for example, by pilots or underwater divers who move from an area of great pressure to one of lower pressure. This causes their intestinal gas to expand, leading to intestinal squeeze. The plain fact is that we must all get rid of this gas by farting, even though the accompanying sound and bad smell may cause embarrassment.

Intestinal gas consists of swallowed air, mixed with what results from the activity of harmless bacteria on poorly digested carbohydrates – carbon dioxide, oxygen, nitrogen, hydrogen and sometimes methane, all of which have no smell. The actual mix of these gases will vary at different times of day in the same individual. In the morning there will be a higher proportion of nitrogen because the hydrogen and carbon dioxide will have been absorbed into the blood during the night. It is less than one per cent of the flatus, consisting of other gases such as hydrogen sulphide, which causes the distinctive smell. Humans can detect hydrogen sulphide itself in concentrations as low as one-half part per billion. In principle, then, foods which have high proportions of nondigestible carbohydrates should be avoided by those who suffer from excessive wind. See *Diet control*. The amount of swallowed air should also be reduced by eating more slowly and avoiding such activities as chewing gum.

An old joke has it that a man who is subject to excessive flatulence mentions it to his doctor. 'I fart all the time,' he tells him. 'I haven't done anything about it because it's not a problem. I break wind silently and there's no smell. For instance, I've farted several times while we've been speaking, but you wouldn't have known it, would you?' The doctor reaches for his prescription pad and starts to write. 'Is this for something to stop my flatulence?' says the patient. 'No,' says the doctor, 'these pills will clear your sinuses so that you get your sense of smell back. And I'll make an appointment for you next week to have a hearing test.'

Joking apart, the American Institute for Preventive Medicine says that if excess flatulence in an individual is accompanied by a severe pain in the abdomen, nausea, or yellowing of the skin or eyes, then a doctor should be consulted at once. Medical advice should also be sought if the flatulence occurs after taking a specific antibiotic. This may have led to bacterial overgrowth in the intestines.

Flatulent fiction

Flatulence sometimes becomes the central theme of a short story. An example, which is made available on the Internet, is *Ill Winds*, by Andrew B. Peterson. A couple (unsubtly anagrammatized as Mr and Mrs Lantfeluce) accuse their neighbour of flatus harassment because he breaks wind at them. His response is that he is only responding in kind, avenging himself for what he has suffered. *Blue Angel*, by L. Collingwood, is another Internet offering in which flatulence figures strongly. There are also novels in which a flatulent scene plays its part (several are quoted in this book), but as yet no full-length novel seems to have been based on an emission of anal gas.

Flatuous

'Flatuous' was the earlier form of 'flatulent'. The associated noun was 'flatuosity'.

Flatuphile

This word was suggested by an Australian correspondent, who assigned the meaning: 'someone who farts when in bed with someone else just for the fun of it'. The term could be used in a more general way of someone who, in suitable circumstances, genuinely enjoys breaking wind. Flatuphile would then apply to most of the world's population.

Flatus

Flatus (rhyming with 'status') has been the medical term for the wind in the stomach or bowels, including that which is expelled through the anus, since the seventeenth century. The layman is more likely to refer to 'wind' or 'gas'. 'Flatus' derives from a Latin word which means 'a blowing, an act of breaking wind', and is ultimately from the Latin *flare*, 'to blow'. The same basic word has given us 'flatulence, flatulency, flatulent', as well as modern neologisms such as 'flatal, flatulate, flatulation, flatulator, flatometer'.

Fluff
······

To 'fluff' is used in some parts of the English-speaking world for 'fart'. Royal Navy slang has 'fluff your pinky' in the sense of 'break wind'. In youthful American slang it is also possible to talk of 'laying a fluffy'. This meaning was no doubt suggested by the idea of actors 'fluffing' – making a mistake – during a performance, or golfers fluffing a shot. 'Fluff' seems not yet to have come to the attention of British lexicographers in this sense.

Fogo
······

'Fogo' was one of the words mentioned to a researcher for the *Dictionary of American Regional English* who asked for words meaning a breaking of wind from the bowels. At first glance 'fogo' looks like a form of 'fogger', which *Webster's Collegiate Dictionary* defines as 'an apparatus for spreading a fog of pesticide'. This would make it a good example of rural humour. However, the word is known to *The Oxford English Dictionary*, which defines it as a 'disagreeable smell, stench'. The editors think that it might be 'arbitrarily formed on the suggestion of 'foh!' the interjection, although they admit the possibility of an association with 'fog'. They cite an 1823 work on slang which glosses 'fogo' as 'the same with a stench'. Another early nineteenth-century source has: 'That word smelt so strong in his nose he had to take out his handkerchief, all scented with musk to get clear of the fogo of it.'

Fowkin
········

An obsolete synonym of 'fart', rarely recorded. An anonymous text of 1600 refers to a man who made his grey mare gallop so fast that 'she let a fowkin fare [go] at the rearward.'

Franklin's prize question

Benjamin Franklin (1706–90), the American states-man, scientist and writer, made a famous contribution to farting lore when he made a spoof proposal to The Royal Academy of Brussels in 1780. His argument may be briefly summarized as follows:

Breaking wind is usually an embarrassment because of the fetid smell that is created. This causes well-bred people to try to retain their wind – a practice which is dangerous to their health. If a means could be found to make exhalations smell pleasant, this would be of great benefit to mankind, of far more practical use than the discoveries of Descartes, Newton, etc. A product is needed that can be mixed with food and which will perfume intestinal gas: indeed, we ought to be able to ask our dinner-guests whether they want our emissions to smell of musk or roses, say, just as we ask them whether they prefer to drink claret or burgundy. Instead of being worried about flatulence, in other words, we should be able to relax in the happy knowledge that we are perfuming the air around us.

It is important to note that Franklin wants the odour of the intestinal gas to be changed while it is still in the body. This may actually be possible. In a posting to an Internet forum, Julian Macassey reported that after eating a lot of candied orange-peel, his farts next morning had a distinctly orangy aroma. Using a spray to try to counteract the smell once it has been expelled can produce a different effect. As someone once said, 'it just smells as if you farted in a flower shop.'

Frequency of emission

It is obviously difficult to say how many times a day the average person breaks wind. The number of occurrences will vary according to age, sex, type of recent food intake, general state of health, and so on. In medical literature the figures often bandied about in this connection are between 14 and 23 escapes a day for the average man, rather less for a woman. In November 1995 the Dutch Liver and Intestine Foundation, which supports research on digestive problems, announced a publicity campaign to encourage people to pass gas 15 times a day for the purposes of intestinal comfort. The fifteenth edition of the *Merck Manual of Diagnosis and Therapy* notes a study of eight normal men, aged 25–35 years, who had an average number of gas passages of 13+ in one day, with an upper limit of 21. It also reports, however, on a study in which one individual farted 141 times in one day, including 70 emissions in a four-hour period.

The Sydney-based gastroenterologist Professor Terry Bolin has pointed out that some men pass small volumes of gas often, while others pass larger volumes less often. The frequency of emission depends on the sensitivity of the walls of the rectum. A man with rectal walls that are sensitive to small amounts of distension will break wind frequently, but the volume of gas expelled each time will be comparatively small. The man whose rectum can tolerate greater distension will pass gas less often, but emit greater quantities. As people age, their bowels become less elastic and more sensitive to distension. Older people may therefore fart more frequently, without actually producing more gas.

In studies where the average number of daily flatulations is being recorded, volunteers are usually given a counter to keep in their pockets which they click every time they break wind. Some researchers prefer to insert a small catheter into the rectum to count emissions. 'Flatographic records', as they have been called, are well established. Charles Darwin, who was subject to 'fits of flatulence' for most of his adult life, made notes in his diaries of their intensity. His comments range from 'almost' and 'barely' through 'rather bad' to 'sharp' and 'excessive'.

A knowledge of what constitutes 'normality' in this domain is obviously necessary for medical practitioners, who can then take note of any exceptional activity. The frequency with which we break wind, along with our temperature, blood pressure, heart-beat, etc., is a useful indication of our general state of health.

In an article called 'Rearing', Tim Rogers amuses himself with statistics. He calculates that of 300 guests who are likely to be at his wedding, 187.5 of them 'will feel the urge to fart in church, during the actual ceremony'. He adds that, given the after-effects of the number of beers he is likely to have drunk the previous evening, 'and the gastrointestinal stress that attends vowing to love someone till death do you part', the chances are rather high that he will be among those 187.5 people.

[Peter Furze kept a flatographic diary for the last three years of his life while he was gathering the materials for the thesis on which this book is based – see the *Preface*. For each emission he made a note not only of the relative loudness and odour, but whether he was alone or in company, indoors or outdoors. If he felt that he had passed more gas than usual in a given period he also made notes of what he had eaten and drunk in the preceding hours. Peter probably wanted to include these

details in his thesis, but I felt that, on the whole, they were not as interesting as Peter seemed to think they were. Just in case anyone wants to know, according to the statistics that Peter himself compiled, he farted on roughly 17,000 occasions in the three-year period. More than 50 per cent of his emissions he rated as foul-smelling, but fortunately he was often on his own when he perpetrated them.]

Friendly comments

Peggy Smith, of Cleveland, Ohio, asked the members of her Public Speaking and Debate class in February, 1997, about their reactions to someone noisily breaking wind. The comments, on the whole, were friendly, ranging from neutral acknowledgment of the act, through concerned enquiries about the culprit's health, to words of congratulation. Typical remarks were: 'Who blew one?' 'Who died?' 'Somebody clapped their cheeks'; 'Check your briefs!' 'Did you hurt anything?' 'Dat's juicy'; 'You a man, for real, chile.'

Similar comments reported from Texas include: 'Son, the next time you eat a skunk, try peelin' it first'; 'Well, your voice has changed, but your breath smells the same'; 'Rave on, Toothless Wonder!'

Gwen Foor, writing in the *Northern Michigan Journal*, describes a standard comment by a long-suffering marital partner: 'For years, the flatulent behaviours of a certain relative (who shall remain nameless) of mine, has sent the youngsters in our clan into fits of hysterical laughter. They run from the room holding their noses, red-faced, arms flailing the air, always hearing the same seven words in that same spousal voice: 'HonEEEEEEEEEEEY, couldn't you have done that OUTsiiiiiiiiide?' and the usual response of: 'Yeeeuuup, but I was in here.'

Fritty

This curious euphemism for 'fart' was mentioned by one American respondent when asked how he referred to 'breaking wind from the bowels'. It no doubt represents a disguised form of the word 'fart' itself, but it also manages to suggest the sizzling sound of a fritter being cooked.

Frogs
•••••

In rural America, a person who has broken wind loudly is said to have 'stepped on a frog' or 'sat on a frog and the frog croaked'. Sometimes there is a  reference to 'mashing frogs'. The fart itself can be described as a 'trodden-on frog'. In a more acceptable version of this saying, from the frog's point of view, a speaker may say merely that 'the frog jumped in the pond'. 'Stepped on a duck' is a variant used by those whose anal noises sound more like quacks than croaks.

Fumigate
•••••••••••

Used humorously to mean 'pass gas in a smelly way'. To fumigate a room with anal gas tends to clear it of people rather than bugs.

Fundamental sigh
••••••••••••••••••••

This is not a quotation from the famous song in *Casablanca*, but Mark Twain's phrase describing a fart. He made use of it in *Some Remarks on the Science of Onanism*, an after-dinner speech delivered to the Stomach Club of Paris:

> Of all the various kinds of sexual intercourse, this [masturbation] has least to recommend it. As an amusement, it is too fleeting; as an occupation, it is too wearing; as a public exhibition, there is no money in it. It is unsuited to the drawing-room, and in the most cultured

society it has long been banished from the social board. It has at last, in our day of progress and improvement, been degraded to brotherhood with flatulence – among the best bred these two arts are now indulged in only in private – though by consent of the whole company, when males only are present, it is still permissible, in good society, to remove the embargo upon the fundamental sigh.

Fyst
·····

This is one possible spelling of a word that was used from the fifteenth to the late eighteenth century to mean a 'foul-smelling fart'. 'Fist' was more frequently used, but this fails to indicate that the word rhymed with 'heist', not 'list' or 'mist'. Other recorded spellings include fyest, fyyst, fiste, fiest, fyste, feist, fice, foist, foyse, foyst. John Skelton uses 'fyest' in *Elynour Rummyng* (1529) when he writes: 'Joan saying she had eaten a fyest; By Christ, said she, thou liest, I haue as sweet a breath as thou.' Cotgrave (1611) uses the phrase 'secrete a fiste'.

Other early literary references emphasize that a fyst was silent, but had an exceptionally strong smell. By the second half of the seventeenth century the exact nature of a fyst was perhaps becoming indistinct, to some writers at least. Charles Cotton writes, in *Scarronides* (1667): 'With that he whistled out most mainly. You might have heard his fist from one side of the sky to the other.' Yet evidence that the 'silent fart' definition lived on is found throughout the eighteenth century. A slang dictionary of 1700 glosses 'foyst' as 'a close strong stink, without noise or report'. Towards the end of the century, in the second edition of his *Classical Dictionary of the Vulgar Tongue*, Francis Grose has an entry for 'fice or foyse – a small windy escape backwards, more obvious to the nose than ears'.

It is not clear how fysts differed from fizzles. Both were originally rather quiet farts, as opposed to the noisy cracks and trumps, but fysts were probably smellier than fizzles. Both words could be used as verbs as well as nouns. 'I must fiddle him till he fyst,' says a character in John Marston's play, *The Dutch*

Courtezan (1605). An eighteenth-century text remarks that one must 'fart and fizzle in the time of need'. What is clear is that our ancestors had a more precise vocabulary at their command, enabling them to describe specific varieties of fart.

Gas

This is the normal layman's term for 'flatus', well used in ordinary speech. Apart from those terms discussed in separate entries (see especially *Pass gas*), typical references include 'breaking gas, gas elimination, gas getting loose, gas in the bowels, gas on the (your) stomach, having gas, leaving gas, making gas, pushing gas'. In *The Naked and the Dead*, Norman Mailer writes: 'they kept loosing gas.' Someone immediately comments: 'Cut out that goddam farting.' 'Gas off' is used as a synonym of 'fart' by some speakers, who might also describe themselves as being 'gassy'.

Gastroenterology

This is the study of the diseases and pathology of the stomach and intestines: gastroenterologists therefore have a professional interest in flatulence and what is associated with it. As a medical man once said: 'Gastroenterologists get very excited at the mere mention of stool.' The word 'gastroenterology' is derived from Greek elements and means 'belly-intestine-science'. The *gas-* at the beginning of the word looks appropriate, but it is coincidentally a part of *gastro-*.

One of the best-known researchers in the field is Dr Michael Levitt, who works at the Veterans Affairs Medical Center, Minneapolis. He has made special studies of how often the average person passes gas, and in what quantities – though in medical language this is referred to as 'flatus frequency' and 'quantity of effluence'. The number of farts per day becomes the number of 'episodes', 'events' or 'intestinal utterances' per day. A witty article by Jeffrey Kluger in *Discover Magazine*, April 1995, said that 'for a medical speciality high in heroism and low in glamour, you can't do much better than gastroenterology.'

Gentlemen and farting

A gentleman is a man who does not fart (audibly) in the presence of women, according to J.P. Donleavy, in *The Ginger Man*. A husband says to his wife: 'I think Kenneth's a gentleman in every respect. Have you ever heard him fart?'

Giggle downunder

Reported as an American (rather than Australian) slang term for a fart.

Global warming

Researchers into global warming have long been taking a suspicious look at the world's livestock population. Cows, for example, are said to break wind every ninety seconds or so, and it has been calculated that 400 quarts of methane a day erupt from each of the 1.2 billion cattle alive at any one time. In his *Cosmic Connection* (1973) C. Sagan was already writing: 'We would not ordinarily consider the flatulence of cattle as a dominant manifestation of life on Earth, but there it is.'

Both methane and carbon dioxide (another major ingredient of cows' emissions) are important greenhouse gases. However, the US Senate recently threw out a proposed amendment to the Clean Air Act which called for a monitoring of methane emissions from various sources, including 'animal production'. Senator Steve Symms of Idaho had said that such an amendment would 'put the nose of the federal government in almost every place it does not belong'.

The attention of scientists has now turned to the gas produced by termites. The British Natural Environment Research Council has announced that termite flatulence may account for as much as 20 per cent of the methane produced annually on earth. The 240 quadrillion termites that are calculated to exist – sixty million for every man, woman and child – release an estimated 176 billion pounds of 'greenhouse gas' per year. This approaches the estimated 224 billion pounds produced by the world's farm livestock.

On a historical note, palaeontologists have wondered whether dinosaurs contributed to their own demise by creating a methane cloud that melted part of the polar icecaps and caused them to drown in the resulting floods.

Gobad's wife
∙∙∙∙∙∙∙∙∙∙∙∙∙∙

There is a traditional Persian folk-tale which concerns the wife of Gobad. It was retold in bowdlerized form as 'The Simpletons' by Anne Sinclair Mehdevi in *Persian Folk and Fairy Tales* (1969):

> Gobad's young wife is very beautiful, but like his parents, she is rather simple. Her head 'is full of butterflies and nonsense'. One day, after a big meal of bean stew, she gives an enormous fart. Just at that moment, the family goat starts to bleat. Gobad's wife thinks that the goat is going to tell her husband and his family about her unfortunate breach of manners. She runs outside and says to the goat: 'Don't tell anyone what happened and I'll give you my earrings and bracelet.' She hangs her earrings on the goat's ears, and wraps her bracelet around the goat's leg. To her delight, the goat stops bleating.
>
> At that moment Gobad's mother appears. She sees the goat wearing the earrings and bracelet and asks her daughter-

in-law what is happening. As the young woman explains why she gave the goat her jewellery, it starts to bleat again. Gobad's mother says: 'O goat, do not ruin this new wife. Say nothing to Gobad and I will give you my speckled dress and my gauze veil.' She runs into the house to get them, then puts them on the goat. Once again, the goat stops bleating.

Now Gobad's father arrives, and demands an explanation in his turn of why the goat is wearing a speckled dress and jewellery. As the two women explain, the goat starts to bleat. Gobad's father gives the goat his new shagreen shoes and implores it to be silent. A little later Gobad's brother arrives, and soon the goat is also wearing a fine turban.

Now Gobad returns from the fields. He asks his family why the goat is dressed in this ridiculous way. The goat begins to bleat, and his mother hastily says: 'O Gobad, do not believe what the goat is saying.' His father says: 'Gobad, stop up your ears.' His brother says: 'The goat is lying.' His young wife bursts into tears.

Gobad is disgusted. 'You're all crazy,' he tells them. 'The goat is bleating because you've forgotten to feed it. I can't stay here and live with you – you're all too simple-minded.' Gobad leaves them and takes to the road. He has many adventures, but wherever he goes, he finds that people are even more stupid than the members of his family. Because

he is intelligent himself, he is able to amass a fortune. Eventually he returns home and enables his wife and family to live a life of ease.

Gone with the wind

This phrase has become the almost invariable heading for any newspaper item that has to do with farting. Mike Farnwald uses the slight variant *Gone With the Winds* for the book of fart cartoons which he advertises on the Internet. When Margaret Mitchell used *Gone With the Wind* as the title for her novel about the American Civil War, she can hardly have guessed that the phrase would become a farting cliché. The novel was published in 1936, selling eight million copies and winning the Pulitzer Prize. Its movie version, starring Vivien Leigh, Clark Gable, Leslie Howard and Olivia de Havilland, was released in 1939 as the longest film ever.

Margaret Mitchell borrowed 'gone with the wind' from a poem by Ernest Dowson, '*Non Sum Qualis Eram*', which begins

with the famous line: 'I have been faithful to thee, Cynara! in my fashion.' Later occurs:

> I have forgot much, Cynara! gone with the wind,
> Flung roses, roses, riotously, with the throng,
> Dancing, to put thy pale, lost lilies out of mind.

In their original context the words are rather beautiful. Lazy sub-editors have tarnished them.

Graffiti

Farts are occasionally the subject of graffiti. A.W. Read's *Classical American Graffiti* (1935), for example, includes:

> Now and then a fart is heard
> Mingling with a dropping turd.

Rather similar is: 'A fart is the cry of an imprisoned turd.' Also from America comes the lavatory-wall question: 'Why did God make farts smell?' The answer is: 'So that the deaf can enjoy them, too.'

Well-known in Britain is the couplet which dates from the time when admission to a cubicle in a public lavatory cost a penny:

> Here sit I, broken-hearted,
> Paid my penny and only farted.

Jack Chambers, of Toronto, says that this circulates in North America attached to a story about 'a Scotsman found dead in a pay-toilet cubicle with a suicide note pinned to his chest'. The note says:

> Here I lie brokenhearted,
> Paid a dime and only farted.

However, these references to paying a penny or a dime probably reflect a cleaned-up version of the original graffito. Allen Walker Read's *Lexical Evidence from Folk Epigraphy in Western North America* (1935) quotes it as it was found in Sentinel, Arizona, on 27 June 1928:

> Here I sit all broken hearted
> Came to shit and only farted.

A less mournful version of this rhyme is:

> Some come to sit and wonder:
> I came to fart and thunder.

A philosophical graffito reported at a web site is: 'It's been a bad week for breaking promises but a good week for breaking wind.' This was signed Contentedly Flatulent.

Grime bubble

An unusual term for a 'fart' reported to the editors of the *Dictionary of American Regional English* in answer to their questionnaire.

Grossology

This is the title of a children's book by Sylvia Branzei, published by Planet Dexter, a satellite of Addison-Wesley, in 1995. It concerns itself with things 'slimy, mushy, stinky, crusty and scaly' in order to explain them in simple scientific terms.

The chapter on farts is both entertaining and informative. Children are told about how often normal people fart and how much gas they expel. They are given a phonetic transcription of the word for 'fart' in languages like Romanian, Japanese, Mandarin Chinese and Taiwanese. They learn about Joseph Pujol (see *Le Pétomane*) and are told about a Japanese 'fartomaniac' who appeared on television in 1980. The latter is said to have farted '3000 times in a row, imitating sounds with his anus'.

More serious information follows, and the children are told how food, having passed from the stomach to the small intestine, enters 'the fart factory' – the large intestine. The bacteria which eat the undigested food at this stage fart themselves, says Ms Branzei, 'so you are just the storage container for the creatures that fart in you'. It is the gas which bacteria have produced which a human being eventually expels.

Ms Branzei comments on the mixture of gases that make up a fart, then ends with child-pleasing suggestions about how to make fart sounds by putting a hand in your armpit and flapping your arm. The book is a highly imaginative and successful approach to getting young children to think about science. In passing it demonstrates how an ordinary fart can have educational value.

Grounds for divorce
....

In upholding a divorce court ruling in 1995, the South Dakota Supreme Court agreed that the fault for the dissolution of the marriage lay clearly with the husband. Among several disturbing patterns of behaviour was the husband's habit of passing gas frequently around the house. When his wife complained he reacted 'testily'. According to the wife, the husband was easily able to regulate the offensive activity and would fart as a 'retaliation thing'. Two court justices dissented on the size of the wife's alimony award, one of them commenting unkindly that the price of gas was going up in Sioux Falls.

Grunt
....

An occasional synonym for 'fart'.

Guinean farts
....

The works of the seventeenth-century physician John Bulwer are quoted over 800 times in *The Oxford English Dictionary*, mainly because Bulwer constantly uses unusual words. In his snappily-titled *Anthropometamorphosis*, published in 1653, he makes comments like 'We in this island do no way like of a shoe-horn-like nose.' More to our purpose, he also mentions that 'The Guineans are very careful not to let a fart.' Especially, no doubt, in the presence of people with shoe-horn-like noses.

Gunshots

A fart is sometimes referred to by the slang term 'tailshot', while a rapid series of anal explosions is commonly compared to the sound of gunshots. In parts of rural America, therefore, someone who is passing gas may be said to be 'shootin' rabbits' or 'shootin' a bunny'. 'Somebody's shootin' rabbits' is typically said when it is not clear who is the offender amongst a group of men. When World War Two was still fresh in the memory, the reference was sometimes changed to 'shootin' Germans'. Similar expressions that have been recorded include the comments that someone has 'shot a cricket' or 'shot a duck'.

Gurk

This is included in a list of slang expressions for 'fart' on an Internet site, but there is no explanation of its origin.

Have the heaves

Reported as an expression meaning 'affected by flatulence'.

He can't fart and chew gum at the same time

This is a well-known comment on the alleged stupidity of an American President. It is what President Lyndon B. Johnson actually said about President Ford, according to R. Reeves, in *A Ford, Not a Lincoln*. The *Bloomsbury Dictionary of Quotations* remarks that it is sometimes quoted as 'Jerry Ford is so dumb that he can't walk and chew gum at the same time.'

He wants to fart higher than his arse

A Frenchman might use the original version of this phrase – *il veut péter plus haut que son cul* – to mean that someone is over-ambitious, and aims too high. Roy Wilder, in *You All Spoken Here*, says that 'he's trying to fart higher than his ass' is used in the same sense in the southern states of America.

He who smelt it, dealt it

A useful comment which can be made when one is accused of having farted. It puts the accuser on the defensive and anticipates his denial, since the full form of the riposte is:

> He who smelt it, dealt it:
> You only deny it if you supply it
> (or 'He who denied it, supplied it.')

An American correspondent says that the couplet can be extended by adding:

> Why fart and waste it,
> When you can burp and taste it.

For some reason there appears to be no feminine version of this saying, though 'she who smelt it, dealt it' is theoretically possible.

History of Farting, The

The title of a paperback by Dr Benjamin Bart, first published in Australia in 1993 by Herron Publications. The British edition was published in 1995 by Michael O'Mara Books. Ardent perdologists will certainly want to add this title to their collection of farting literature.

. . . .

It is known that Adolf Hitler suffered from flatulence, and some reports say that when he left the room there was a rush to open the windows. In this connection, it is also often said that Hitler was a vegetarian, but Richard H. Schwartz, author of *Judaism and Vegetarianism*, points out that although Hitler would occasionally go on vegetarian binges 'to cure himself of excessive sweatiness and flatulence', his main diet was meat-centred. Other Hitler biographers such as Robert Payne and Albert Speer agree. They talk about Hitler's predilection for such non-vegetarian foods as Bavarian sausages, ham, liver and game.

Fred C. McKenzie, in his book *The Greatest Illusion: The Death(?) of Adolf Hitler*, says that Hitler's flatulence indirectly supports the view that the German leader escaped from Berlin in 1945 and was sheltered by General Franco in Madrid. In May 1945 Franco's medical staff suddenly ordered from Spain's largest pharmaceutical company a carton of 144 bottles of Doctor Koster's Anti-Gas Pills, repeating the order on a

monthly basis until October 1947. By 1945 Hitler was known to be swallowing these pills by the handful, having become addicted to the strychnine that was in them. McKenzie puts forward much other evidence to back his claim that the pills were for Hitler, and that the

body in Berlin was that of a 'double'. He believes that Hitler in fact died in Madrid in 1947.

The 'rush to open the windows' when Hitler left the room sounds suspiciously like war-time propaganda, similar to taunts which insisted that 'Schicklgruber' was Hitler's real surname (it wasn't). If the accusation was a fabrication, it is nevertheless interesting that spreading a rumour that someone was a smelly farter played its part in an early dirty-tricks campaign.

Honking

The honking of low-flying geese is sometimes offered as the explanation of what was actually a noisy emission of gas. 'Honk' itself is used in slang for 'break wind' or a 'breaking of wind'. Sometimes an allusion is made to the honking of a motor horn rather than geese, as in the coarse definition of a fart: 'a turd honking for the right of way'. *Honk* is also said to be the name of a magazine circulated to members of the Old Farts Car Club. See also *Beef*.

Horsed

London market traders are likely to say that someone has 'horsed', meaning that he has farted. The allusion is to Cockney rhyming slang, where 'horse and cart' is used for 'fart'. By tradition the second half of the rhyming couplet is dropped in speech. The same traders may well quote the well-known:

> Have a good fart
> It's good for your heart.

HotBot

This is the appropriate name of a search engine which can be used to find fart-based web sites. As it happens, it was much used by Peter Furze when he was doing the research for the thesis on which *Tailwinds* is based – see the *Preface*.

I don't trust my arse with a fart

A remark likely to be made by someone suffering from diarrhoea.

Immaculate farting

In *Dubin's Lives*, Bernard Malamud describes a woman who is, as are countless of her ilk, keenly sensitive to bad smells. Especially interesting is Malamud's comment on how she deals with farting: 'She was assailed by the smell of decaying things: food in the refrigerator, old shoes, old clothes, old closets. A close room compelled her, gasping, to throw open a window. A whiff of cheap perfume in a crowd set her teeth on edge. Kitty disliked body odours – abolished her own, kept Dubin informed of his. She passed gas immaculately; after an emission by him she sincerely asked what the smell was.'

Sylvia Goldberg, by contrast, in Howard Jacobson's *Coming From Behind*, is worried about unpleasant noises. 'The hell of being human was not alleviated, for her, simply by becoming invisible – there was also the problem of being *heard*.' This lady, Jacobson tells us, 'knew of no greater or more urgent service to perform than to save her family from all the horrors of the body: to disguise her own and to silence theirs. One tiny sneaking misdirected inadvertent little fart – and all would have been up with the Goldbergs!'

Indian flatulence

Khushwant Singh, in *Delhi, a Novel*, writes: 'Indians have a very poor sense of humour and treat farting as a topic of jest. Since they eat highly spiced *tamasik* foods, they are the world's champion farters and have much occasion to laugh at each other. Once a Minister of Cabinet recording a talk for the External Services of All India Radio let out a Trumpet. The talk had to be re-recorded. However, when the time came, by mistake, the original recording was put on the air. It gave an Indian the unique distinction of having his fart heard around the world.'

The 'unique distinction' that Singh talks about has in fact become rather commonplace now that the web makes it possible to listen to farts from all parts of the globe. Several web sites offer a selection of recorded fart noises, and invite contributors to send in their own efforts.

Inflatable lady

Kenneth Williams reports in one of his diary entries that someone had told him a 'mildly amusing story about a man coping with a plastic inflatable dummy lady [made by the Japanese for intercourse]'. Perhaps the story wasn't told very well, since the punch-line is a strong one. 'I was just biting her neck when she suddenly farted and flew out of the window.'

International contest

A recording of the First International Crepitation Contest is one of the items advertised in Johnson Smith's catalogue *Things You Never Knew Existed*. It is said to have been put together in the 1950s by 'some zany radio personalities', and to feature the English champion Lord Windesmere of Whopping Foxhole against the American challenger, cabbage-loving Paul Boomer. Versions of it are available at several sites on the Internet.

The Johnson Smith catalogue offers several other fart-associated products. Fart putty, when pushed into a cup, is said to create 'gaseous sounds so graphic, they ought to be illegal'. There is a Hoof Arted baseball cap, and 'high-tec, state of the art electronic replacements' for the traditional whoopee cushions. One of these flatus surrogates can be controlled by a radio transmitter, while the so-called 'fart machine' can be set to make its embarrassing noise after a pre-determined time has elapsed. The Johnson Smith Company operates from Bradenton, Florida.

Interpreting a fart

Philip Roth, in *Portnoy's Complaint*, is describing a psychiatrist when he says: 'Sometimes he coughs, sometimes he grunts, sometimes he belches, once in a while he farts, whether voluntarily or not who knows, though I hold that a fart has to be interpreted as a negative transference reaction on his part.' This comment about fart-interpretation is a reminder that no one seems to have invented a system of divination based on farting, on a par with cartomancy, cheiromancy, logomancy, necromancy, pyromancy, xylomancy and the like. There is clearly scope for someone to set up a school of perdomancy, 'divination of a person's character and future by means of his or her farts'.

Intestinal distress

A polite reference to an attack of flatulence.

Italian farts

Beroalde de Verville tells the following story in *The Way of Succeeding*:

The Lord of Lierne, a French gentleman, went to bed with a prostitute in Rome. As these ladies well know their business, Imperia – for that was the prostitute's name – had previously obtained some little pellicles, filled by perfumers with a strong scent. With a supply of these within reach, and holding the gentleman in her arms, Imperia allowed herself to be loved. To add an edge to the love-play, and to please her lover even more, Imperia took one of the pellicles in her hand and burst it at a suitable moment, thus making the audible sound of a fart.

On hearing this the gentleman hastily withdrew his head from the bed to give himself air. 'It's not what you think,' said Imperia. 'You must experience it before being afraid.' Thus persuaded, her lover buried his head again in the bed-clothes and received an agreeable odour quite contrary to what he had expected. He savoured it with pleasure. After this sequence of events had been repeated a number of times, the Lord of Lierne enquired of Imperia if such winds proceeded from her, given that they smelt so good. Similar winds emanating from the lower portions of French ladies, he said, were stinking and abominable. To this Imperia replied to the effect that Italian ladies, due to the nature of their country and its aromatic foods, and because they made much use of sweet-smelling articles, produced their quintessence in the lower regions as if it were the neck of a retort. 'In truth,' said the Frenchman, 'our own ladies fart in quite a different way.'

It so happened that after some more cracking of pellicles, because she held her wind for too long, Imperia farted naturally, substantially and at length. The Lord of Lierne diligently stuck his nose under the sheets in order to appreciate the good odour, which he wished to savour to the full. But he was deceived; he received through his nose a stench of barnyard proportions. 'Oh, my dear lady,' he said, 'what have you done?' She answered, 'My lord, I was but paying you a compliment. I wanted to remind you of your own country.'

A saying reported from southern Italy is: *Quando il malato scoppia, il medico plange* – 'When the sick man farts, the doctor cries.' It is not clear why the doctor cries, unless the patient's emissions are especially foul. In that case the saying might be rendered: 'A fart a day keeps the doctor away'.

Japanese farts
....

Dr Daniel Long, an American who teaches in Japan, reports that 'the Japanese are often amazed that Americans will blow their noses at the dinner-table, yet those same Americans are shocked when Japanese fart there. In America, farting is worse (mannerwise) than belching, but my 14 years in Japan have given me the impression that it is not perceived as any worse here. Just unpleasant (because of the smell), but not particularly bad manners.' The Japanese, no doubt, consider that blowing one's nose is something that can be controlled. The person concerned has the option of leaving the room to do it. Breaking wind is more likely to be involuntary.

Dr Long adds: 'In Japanese "fart" is *onara* or *he*, with the verb being *he wo koku* or *onara wo suru*. There is an expression *he de mo nai* – 'it's not even a fart' – which criticizes something or somebody as being insignificantly small, playing an insignificantly small role in things.' The Japanese proverb – *He o hitte shiri tsubome* – 'no use scrunching your buttocks after a fart' – is the equivalent of 'no use closing the stable door after the horse has bolted'.

The Japanese are in some ways more preoccupied with bodily functions than the Anglo-Saxons. There is a children's book by Shinta Cho, *Onara – a story of farts* which has been on sale in Japan since 1978. The American version, translated by Amanda Mayer Stinchecum, is entitled *The Gas We Pass* and was published by Kane/Miller Book Publishers, New York, in 1994. It mainly consists of pictures, but the text gives children a basic explanation of why they fart, why some farts smell worse than others, why farts should not be held back, and so on. The book ends with a word which is presumably an original contribution from the translator: 'Fartheewell'. See also *Grossology* and *Ninja fart*.

A joke related to Japanese farting runs as follows. A man visits his doctor and says that something strange is happening to him: when he farts it always sounds like H-o-n-d-a-a-a. The doctor is puzzled, but thinks to himself: 'Honda – that's a

Japanese name, maybe my Japanese colleague will be able to help.' He calls his colleague, who immediately says: 'Check the patient's teeth.' The doctor does so and discovers that the patient has an abscess. He advises him to go to a dentist, and not to worry about the strange-sounding farts.

When the doctor next sees the patient he learns that the H-o-n-d-a-a-a farts stopped when the abscess was cured. The doctor decides to telephone his Japanese colleague to congratulate him on the successful conclusion to his diagnosis. 'But how did you know that he had an abscess?' he asks. 'Nothing to it,' says his Japanese colleague. 'I remembered that old medical saying: "Abscess makes the fart go H-o-n-d-a-a-a."'

Jonsonian farts

Shakespeare avoided the word 'fart', but Ben Jonson had no qualms about using it. It is one of the first words heard in *The Alchemist*, as Subtle tells Face: 'I fart at thee.' In Act Two, Sir Epicure Mammon refers to 'my poets, the same that writ so subtly of the fart, whom I shall entertain still for that subject'. In *Bartholomew Fair* Nightengale sings a ballad in which there is a reference to 'the windmill blown down by the witch's fart'.

Joyous fart

This interesting concept is referred to in the German saying *aus einem traurigen Arsch fährt kein fröhlicher Furz* – 'no joyous fart comes from a sad arse'. The meaning is that you can expect nothing cheerful to emerge from a sad situation. No nonsense about every cloud having a silver lining, it seems, to the German way of thinking.

Kwatz
·······

The Fart Fact Page on the Internet mentions 'kwatz' as a slang term for a breaking of wind, but the word has not been found elsewhere.

Latin farts
···········

A Classics scholar reports that 'the (more malodorous) Latin word for the verb "fart" is *pedere* (*pedo, is, pepedi*), and is so used by Catullus and Horace. The participle *peditum* is also used as a noun. The less offensive word is *crepare* (*crepo, as, ui, itum*), which has a basic sense of "crackle" or "squeak". It is used by Cato, in reference to a controversy concerning ill-omened farts, and by Plautus.'

Laughing

As with a fit of coughing, laughing heartily can sometimes make a person fart. If one happens to be heavily pregnant when laughing, the fart is almost inevitable. Elaine Feinstein makes the point in *The Amberstone Exit*, where the opening scene is set in a labour ward: 'When Emily asked her whether she thought anyone could hold a baby back just by wishing it, she laughed until she farted under the sheets.' See also *Scape*.

Lay a fart

An American variant of 'let a fart'. Bill King, writing from Arizona, wonders whether 'lay one' can be 'traced to some influential linguistic/immigrant group', since 'let one' was almost certainly the original form. He also suggests that the 'lay' version of the saying 'is a comical analogy to a hen laying an egg [and perhaps the subsequent cackling]'. In American slang 'lay heat' is one of the euphemisms for 'fart' that crops up on the Internet.

Let off

A number of contemporary slang terms for 'fart' begin with 'let', which represents an interesting linguistic survival from medieval times. Chaucer's usual expression was 'let flee a fart'. Modern terms include 'let a crack, let a fart, let a poop, let a slipper, let a windy, let off air, let gas, let off, let off some gas, let off some wind, let off steam, let one fly, let it go, let one go, let one loose, let one off, let one rip, let it rip, let one slip out, let a smelly, let it out, let a stinker (or stinko), let out air, let wind, let your air go.' Some speakers refer merely to having 'let one'.

Lift a leg

An occasional euphemistic synonym for 'fart', though the phrase conjures up the image of a dog urinating. See *Warnings* for a reference to raising a leg as the sign of an impending fart.

Light it up

A synonym for 'fart' currently in use amongst American students. Perhaps there is an allusion to the once dangerous, though popular, habit of setting light to a fart. See also *Methane*.

Losing your manners

This interesting euphemism for 'farting' was mentioned when informants were asked to tell the editors of the *Dictionary of American Regional English* how they referred to 'breaking wind from the bowels'.

Love farts

The extraordinary statement that love can be compared to a fart was made by Sir John Suckling (1609–42) in his poem '*Love's Offence*'. His argument runs:

> Love is the fart
> Of every heart,
> It pains a man when kept close,
> And others doth offend, when 'tis let loose.

Low flying geese!

This phrase is used by some speakers to explain the noise of a loud fart, the allusion being to the honking of a gaggle of geese. A more complex idea is raised by the web site devoted to the baritone Leo Kottke. This says that Kottke's voice has long been likened to 'geese farts on a muggy day'. The author of the web page chooses to examine at length 'the foolishness of comparing the sound generated by the vocal chords of a human being to that of gas escaping from the rear orifice of a waterfowl', and goes on to question whether geese do actually fart. A search of ornithological works, it seems, has failed to reveal any evidence of anserine, or any other avian, farts. Even if geese do pass gas in an audible way, says the web site article, the 'muggy day' reference is still unacceptable: 'A humidified goose poot would be quieter than usual.'

Lust killer

The average man or woman finds it difficult to think about sexual activity when distracted by intestinal gas. As Khushwant Singh says in *Delhi, a Novel*: 'Anyone who suffers from wind knows that until expelled, it will not allow the flame of lust to be kindled.' Singh describes a young man who is waiting for a woman to join him. He knows that she will expect him to make love to her, but he has 'a balloon full of wind' in his stomach instead of lust in his loins. He cannot pass gas, even though he hops around the room on one leg or lies on his back with his knees pressed into his paunch, both apparently ways in which to release wind from the stomach. The young man has no desire for sex; instead he prays 'for a long, satisfying fart.'

Luther, Martin

Martin Luther (1483–1546) was the German leader of the Protestant Reformation. His learned collaborator, Melanchthon, says that when Luther encountered the Devil and overcame him in an argument, 'the Demon departed indignant and murmuring to himself, after having emitted a crepitation [fart] of no small size, which left a train of foul odour in the chamber for several days afterwards.' The association of the Devil with an evil, sulphurous smell has of course persisted through the centuries, though it is not usually explained in terms of the Devil's farting. On another occasion Luther revenged himself for this diabolic 'farting shot' by using the same weapon. Doctrinal arguments had not been enough in themselves to overcome the Devil, but Luther says that he did so *mit einem Furz*, 'with a fart'.

Luther was known for his direct manner and rough and ready speech. His remark *Warum rülpset und pfurzet Ihr nicht? Hat es Euch nicht geschmecket?* is often quoted in Germany. An English rendering is: 'Why do you not belch and fart? Wasn't the meal to your taste?' Robert Browning seems to have Luther's farting comments in mind when he wrote:

> Grand rough old Martin Luther
> Bloomed fables – flowers or furze,
> The better the uncouther:
> Do roses stick like burrs?

The reference to 'furze' can hardly be a coincidence – *die Fürze* in German is the plural form of 'fart.'

Maintaining illusions

A girl who wants to get her man must be especially careful about farting, according to *How to Marry the Man of Your Choice*, by Margaret Kent. The author tells her female readers: 'If you need to pass gas, excuse yourself from his presence. Try not to destroy illusions by unpleasant odours. If you need to pass gas, face him.'

Make a thunderclap out of a fart

This is the literal translation of the German phrase *aus einem Furz einen Donnerschlag machen*. In English it is normally rendered by the much duller 'make a mountain out of a molehill.' The thunderclap-fart reference surfaces in *Portnoy's Complaint*, by Philip Roth: 'Once a month my father took me down with him to the *shvitz* bath. . . . If it were not for the abrupt thunderclap of a fart, or the snores sporadically shooting up around me like machine-gun fire, I would believe we were in a morgue.'

Marital farts

'Next to him in bed Clare shifted and sighed. There was a muffled fart under the blankets. She raised herself on her elbow and leaned over her husband to look at the clock. The smell of her wind mingled with the liverish, early-morning odour from her mouth'.

Piers Paul Read, *A Married Man*

Martial farts

Those who practise the martial arts attempt to unify the mind and body. However, it seems that the delivery of a kick or punch, or any similar violent movement, may lead to a breaking of wind. This in turn can affect an individual's concentration and perhaps leave him exposed to an effective counter attack. The acceptance of a fart as a natural act of the body, giving no cause for embarrassment or discomfort, is therefore said to be particularly essential for those who seek inner tranquillity. Some would say that this statement applies to all of us.

Matters of etiquette

The fifteenth-century 'Handbook of Good Manners', *Urbanitatis*, instructs its young readers on such matters as doffing their caps before a lord, and not spitting or blowing their noses. It then continues: 'Be privy of voydance and lette hit go.' 'Voydance' would normally have to do with evacuating the bowels, but since it is unlikely that a young person, however inexperienced in the ways of the world, would do this while addressing a nobleman, the meaning here is probably: 'Fart if you must but do it discreetly.'

Two centuries later, Petrie's *Rules of Good Deportment* (1720) remarks that 'it is rude in company to break wind any manner of way, even when you are amongst inferiors'. More recent works on etiquette appear to agree with this basic principle, though few now dare to speak about being 'amongst inferiors.' They advise you to leave the room, or at least move away from a group of people, if you think you are about to break wind.

Frank McCourt, in his novel *Angela's Ashes*, mentions another unwritten rule about when one does not fart. Young Frank has typhoid, and Dr Campbell is sitting by the bed. 'The doctor's eyes close and he snores a little. He tilts over on the chair and farts and smiles to himself and I know now I'm going to get better because a doctor would never fart in the presence of a dying boy.'

Etiquette frowns severely on breaking wind in rather more commonplace circumstances. For example, it is not good form to fart in an automobile, unless you are the driver and have no passengers. In those circumstances you are allowed to fart to your heart's content, and most drivers – male and female – do so. When there are passengers, it is essential that gas emissions are avoided by all concerned, especially on a cold or rainy day when the windows are closed.

Much the same rule applies to elevators. You can break wind if alone (though you may get caught out – see *Painting the elevator*), but if other people are present, the emission of a pungent smell should be avoided. J.P. Donleavy, in *The Unexpurgated Code*, likens the elevator fart to the one which is laid in the 'airless conditions encountered on tightly crowded public transport'. In both cases no immediate escape is possible for those who are nearby.

There is a joke related to farting etiquette which concerns an elderly English couple in a pub. When a man sitting near them farts loudly, the elderly Englishman admonishes him: 'Sir, do you realize that you have just broken wind before my wife?' The other man replies: 'Sorry, old bean, I didn't realize it was her turn.'

Meaty farts

The opening sentences of Nadine Gordimer's short story *Spoils* are: 'In the warmth of the bed your own fart brings to your nostrils the smell of rotting flesh; the lamb chops you devoured last night. Seasoned with rosemary and with an undertaker's paper-frill on the severed rib-bones. Another corpse digested.'

Metaphorical farting

The word 'fart' is sometimes used metaphorically of a non-human noise that resembles a fart. In *A Cack-Handed War*, for example, Edward Blishen writes: 'A few days later I crept into Bob Doyle's lorry as he took it farting and hiccoughing towards the gate.' Henry Miller's *Tropic of Cancer* has: 'Nothing can be more harassing, more nerve-racking, than the sound of a French orchestra. Particularly one of those lugubrious female orchestras with everything coming in squeaks and farts, with a dry algebraic rhythm and the hygienic consistency of toothpaste.'

Methane

A common misconception is that the gas produced by human beings is composed entirely of methane. In fact, methane only forms part of the intestinal gas which is expelled through the rectum in about one adult person in three. Children produce no methane at all until they reach their teens. Experts say that an easy way for an individual to ascertain whether methane is present in his or her own flatus is to look in the toilet bowl. If methane is trapped in a person's stools they will be lighter than water and will float.

When it *is* present in a gas emission, methane is odourless but inflammable, as many a schoolboy has discovered by means of practical experiment. Will Self, in *My Idea of Fun*, recalls: 'At Varndean some boys could set light to their farts.' Charles Beowe also reports: 'I had a college roommate who would sometimes light his fart, sending a tongue of flame as many as three feet away from his body. Once one flashed back on him, however, badly burning his perineum. He later became a physician, but I don't think that alone was the reason.'

The *Winnipeg Free Press* recently commented on this subject: 'Then there are the blue angels that were famous in the youth culture of the 1950s and 1960s. "Blue angels" was a nickname given to bluish flames created by blowing wind and igniting it with a flame to create special visual effects with flatus.' The short story *Blue Angel*, which L. Collingwood makes available on the Internet, confirms the terminology: 'If it hadn't been for John Patrick McGuinness, the whole front row of Sister Loyola's 6th grade Latin class would never have mastered the art of fart lighting. That is how we got the nickname, the Blue Angels, on account of the incredible blue flame we inspired, and often on command.'

Frank McCourt tops all this in *Angela's Ashes*, where Pa Keating relates that he 'solved one of the great problems of trench warfare. In the trenches it was so wet and muddy they had no way of boiling the water for the tea. He said to himself, Jasus, I have all this gas in my system and 'tis a great pity to waste it. So he shoved a pipe up his arse, lit a match to it, and there in a second he had a fine flame ready to boil water in any billycan. Tommies came running from trenches all around when they heard the news and they gave him any amount of money if he'd let them boil water.'

Much was made of the explosive potential of fart-methane in *The Nutty Professor*, a movie starring Eddie Murphy in its re-made, superior version. In one scene, after a gargantuan meal has been followed by much passing of wind, Murphy is heard to say, 'Don't nobody light a match.' This warning goes unheeded, with dire results. (Peter Furze had presumably not seen this movie. Had he done so, he would no doubt have exercised more caution when he conducted his own fatal experiment with fart-methane – see the *Preface*.)

The Club Methane site on the Web attributes the success of Wernher von Braun's work on rockets to an accidental happening in his laboratory. His laboratory assistant, Hildegarde, 'after a luncheon of bratwurst and lager', was bending to sweep up a broken test tube when she expelled gas. This was ignited by a nearby bunsen burner and gave Wernher his great idea. It was a case of a fart having a profound effect on the history of mankind, according to Stephen Merrill, who maintains the site. This particular tale is unusual in that it mentions a woman's fart being ignited, albeit accidentally. It is invariably males who deliberately indulge in this practice, though gastroenterologists report that women's farts are in fact more likely to contain methane than those of men.

On a more serious note, medical history records many instances of explosions that have occurred in a patient's colon during an operation. Methane which has been present there has been ignited by use of a cauterizer, or as a medical source prefers to express it, the explosions have usually been 'triggered by the use of electrocauterization performed through a proctosigmoidoscope. Many of these cases occurred when mannitol, a fermentable carbohydrate, was used as a purgative to cleanse the colon.' The same source adds that 'use of non-fermentable cleansing agents has virtually eliminated this kind of accident.'

'Miller's Tale, The'

The most famous literary reference to farting occurs in Chaucer's 'The Miller's Tale', one of *The Canterbury Tales*. The story concerns John, a well-off, elderly carpenter; Alison, his attractive eighteen-year-old wife; Nicholas, a young student of astrology who is the carpenter's lodger, and Absalon, the parish clerk. Absalon loves dancing, playing his fiddle, and visiting all the local inns to flirt with the barmaids, 'but sooth to seyn,'

says Chaucer, 'he was somdel squaymous of fartyng' – curiously, he was rather squeamish in the matter of farting. This is worthy of note, since Chaucer's contemporaries saw nothing to be squeamish about in such a natural act.

Both Absalon and Nicholas the lodger are very keen to get Alison into bed. Where Nicholas is concerned, she is not unwilling, but tells him that they will have to be careful because her husband is a very jealous man. Her husband is also very gullible, since he believes Nicholas when he says that his astrological studies have revealed that there is about to be another Noah's Flood. To survive it, Nicholas says, the three of them must shelter in separate tubs, hung from the roof. No one else must be told what is to happen, and on the night of the flood itself, they must all remain completely quiet. John agrees to all this, and on the night that the flood is due, conceals himself in his tub and begins to pray. Alison and Nicholas sneak off to bed and enjoy a night of love.

Absalon, as it happens, believes John to be away from home that night and decides to visit Alison. He appears outside her window before dawn and tells her how much he loves her. When Alison tells him to go away, he demands at least a kiss. Alison whispers to Nicholas, who is still in bed with her, that they might as well have a laugh. She opens the window, but instead of putting her face out to be kissed, she thrusts out her backside. It is still pitch dark, and Absalon bestows a loving kiss on what he thinks are her lips. It then occurs to him that ladies do not normally have beards, yet he is kissing something 'al rough and long y-herd', all rough and hairy. Alison shuts the window, and Absalon hears her and Nicholas having a good laugh at his expense. He vows to get his revenge.

A little later Absalon once again appears at Alison's window. He says he has brought her a golden ring which he will give her in exchange for another kiss. Nicholas thinks the previous joke can be improved, and this time it is he who sticks his buttocks out of the window. 'Speak to me,' says Absalon, 'I don't know where you are.' There follow the famous lines:

> This Nicholas anon let flee a fart,
> As greet as it had been a thunder-dent,
> That with the strook he was almost y-blent.

Nicholas lets fly a fart like a thunder-clap, and it almost blinds poor Absalon.

This time, however, Absalon has come prepared. He has borrowed a red-hot iron from the local smithy and thrusts it into the middle of Nicholas's rump. The young student screams for 'Water, water!' In his tub under the roof, John the carpenter hears the cries and thinks that the flood has duly arrived.

Chaucer's tale is written in the English of the fourteenth century, which creates difficulties for the modern reader. Translations into modern English are readily available, one of the best being that of Nevill Coghill, first published in 1951 and available as a Penguin Classic.

Mink
••••••

'Mink' is used as a euphemism for 'fart' in some parts of rural America, no doubt because the animal has a reputation for being rather smelly.

Misunderstanding

A story that circulates in various forms (recounted, for instance, by Kenneth Williams in *Acid Drops*) concerns an official visit to Britain by an African leader. He was accorded all the usual honours, including a procession through London in horse-drawn carriages. The Queen, in the leading landau with the African visitor, was rather taken aback when one of the horses farted very loudly, but offered a gracious apology: 'I'm awfully sorry about that, Mr President. Most unfortunate.' The African dignitary was equally gracious. 'That's quite all right, your Majesty. Indeed, until you spoke I thought it was the horse.'

A version of this anecdote that can be found on the Internet says that the African leader was General Yakubu Gowan, the Nigerian dictator, on a state visit to Britain in 1966.

Musical instruments

Fart noises are often compared to the sounds made by musical instruments. The trumpet is most often mentioned, with 'trump' having become well established as a euphemism for a loud anal emission. 'Bugling' and 'blowing one's horn' are similarly used. The Indian novelist, Khushwant Singh, compares other exhalations with the *shehnai*, a wind instrument of the oboe class, the opening sounds of a Scottish bagpipe, and the *tabla*, a pair of Indian drums played by hand. Tim Rogers, in his article 'Rearing', refers to the 'meek, piccolo noise' made by his future mother-in-law when she forgot herself momentarily and farted in his presence. He adds that his own father was far more strident, as if he were 'the actual boogie-woogie bugle boy of Company B of whom the Andrews sisters sang'.

Mysterious words

Various lists exist of words used for breaking wind from the bowels. One of the most wide-ranging is that of the *Dictionary of American Regional English*, compiled after researchers had gone out into the field to question informants. Other lists are made available on the Internet. The latter usually represent an individual's collections of words, with occasional contributions from others. In nearly every list at least one mysterious word seems to occur, unknown to any of the other list-compilers, or for that matter, to lexicographers. Sometimes the word itself is familiar, but there is no known connection with flatulation.

Examples of such words from the DARE list include *buncil* and *punt*. 'Buncil' defeats the dictionaries. The word 'punt' is of course well established, but it is difficult to see how it can relate to breaking wind. Another puzzling word occurs in *Wind Breaks*, the little book in which the Australian authors Professor Terry Bolin and Rosemary Stanton discuss flatulence. This work has a short list of euphemisms for 'fart' as an appendix, one of them being 'braff'. The term is as unknown to dictionaries and to all other writers on the subject as 'boop', which occurs at one of the web sites. Both words may merely be onomatopoeic; only those who invented them know.

Nature and nurture

A quote from Tim Rogers, in his article called 'Rearing' which he makes available on the Internet: 'While nature largely determines the tenor of our farts, nurture dictates how we deal with them.'

Ninja fart

This is a modern term, referring to the characteristics of a Ninja, a Japanese warrior trained in *ninjutsu*, the art of stealth or invisibility. A Ninja fart therefore describes a silent exhalation which has a deadly odour. The success of the film and television cartoon series *Teenage Mutant Ninja Turtles* in the late 1980s made English-speakers aware of the Japanese word.

Noble gas

This description is applied by chemists to gases such as helium, neon, argon, krypton and xenon, all of which are especially stable. In the language of flatulence, 'noble gas' is used to describe a fart which has no smell.

Non-farters, the

In Margaret Atwood's novel *Alias Grace*, Grace Marks and Mary Whitney are young servant-girls in Canada in the early 1840s. At one point Grace thinks to herself: 'People dressed in a certain kind of clothing are never wrong. Also they never fart. What Mary Whitney used to say was, If there's farting in a room where they are, you may be sure you done it yourself. And even if you never did, you better say so or it's all Damn your insolence, and a boot in the backside and out on the street with you.'

Nun's fart

This refers to a rather delicious fart, one that can be eaten. 'Nun's fart' is the literal translation of French *pet de nonne*, the name of a fritter made with choux pastry.

Old farts
··········

Old Fart is the brand name of a strong bottled ale, sold in Britain. It joins a number of other bottled beers which are meant to have a curiosity value because of their slightly outrageous names. Americans may not be able to enjoy this drink, but they can at least join The Old Farts Club of America, based at 41 Crossroads Plaza, Suite 101, West Hartford, Connecticut 06117. Individuals know that they are eligible for membership, according to the club's announcement on the Internet, if they complain to the waitress that the gazpacho is cold, walk into a room but forget why they went there, and so on. Members receive a baseball cap which proclaims that they are official old farts along with their certificate of membership and credit-card-style membership card.

(I was surprised to discover that Peter Furze, on whose research this book is based – see the *Preface* – was an honorary member of the OFC of America. Peter must have been by far their youngest recruit, though perhaps being an old fart is a matter of mentality rather than physical age. Though still in his twenties, Peter was in some ways more of an old fart in his attitude than some men in their seventies. Anyway, his honorary membership of the Club must have given him great pleasure. It was almost as if his devoted study of farting lore and language had caused him to become a fart.)

As an expression of contempt, 'old fart' seems to have come into use in the 1960s. 'What does the silly old fart want?' occurs in J. Sangster's 1968 novel *Touchfeather*. The magazine *Ink* reported in 1971 that Marty Feldman, leaving the witness

Leslie A. Dunkling, a member of the Old Farts Club of America

stand, had said of the judge: 'I don't think he even knew I was here, the boring old fart.' The most boring old farts of all are likely to object strongly to being described as such. When Will Carling, captain of the England rugby team in 1996, referred to the administrators of the sport as 'a bunch of old farts', he was forced to make a public apology. As it happens, 'you old fart' would probably have seemed a fairly mild vocative in the seventeenth century. A typical insult by a Jonsonian character was 'you whoreson foist, you'. (See *Fyst.*)

'Old' is sometimes used affectionately, as in 'old chap', 'old mate', but in this instance the implication is that being aged over fifty, say, automatically makes one a worthless person. That worthlessness is probably the only sense the speaker has in mind when he refers to someone as 'an old fart'. He is not necessarily implying that the person concerned farts more than anyone else, though as it happens, farting frequency does tend to increase with age – see *Frequency of emission.*

S.J. Perelman demonstrated that laughing at it is another method of dealing with the 'old fart' accusation. *Don't Tread on*

Me, a selection of his letters, contains one written to Ronald Searle, on 5 August 1971, when Perelman was living in Onslow Square. He says: 'To see me with my shopping bag in the Old Brompton Road, picking up an egg at Oakeshott's, a brioche in Bute Street, and a bunch of radishes at Leguma is to see a typical South Kensington old fart. "There goes a typical South Kensington old fart," is a comment oft-heard around the tube station.'

In the world of computers, 'old fart' has the special meaning of a kind of tribal elder. Computer buffs say that 'it has become a title self-assumed with remarkable frequency by Usenetters who have been programming for more than about 25 years and often appears attached to Jargon File contributions of great archeological significance.' 'Old fart', then, is usually a term of insult in the second or third person but can be one of pride when used in the first person.

Opening the lunchbox

This phrase is a synonym for farting reported from Australia. It was made known to British readers in the 1960s by a cartoon strip in *Private Eye* magazine. The reference was presumably to the smells that emerge from cheese and other foods that are inside the lunchbox.

Operatic farting

An article in *The Times* of London (25 October 1996) by Philip Hensher, said that 'idle gossip has it that the stellar cast of one very grand opera production currently running in London are at complete loggerheads, owing to the soprano's unbreakable habit of farting at precisely the same point in the second act.'

In one sense there is nothing unusual in this, since there seems to be a well-established theatrical tradition that performers fart loudly while on stage, whether singing, speaking or dancing. What is more noteworthy is the willingness of *The Times*'s sub-editor to allow farting to be called, for once, by its proper name.

Oppedere

This Latin verb meant 'to fart at someone', in the sense of 'deride, mock or insult' that person. At one time it was imitated in English. Thus, one of the opening lines of Ben Jonson's play *The Alchemist* (1610), as Face and Subtle come on to the stage, is 'I fart at thee!' Perhaps at this point the actor is supposed to blow a raspberry. As it happens, there is also a German phrase *auf etwas furzen*, literally 'to fart at something', though a better translation of this would be 'not to give a fart, not to care a jot about something'.

Organ arse

An Australian term for someone who frequently and deliberately farts in the presence of other people.

Owning up

The normal rule about taking the blame for a fart is – don't, unless you really have no choice. Blaming another person or animal in the vicinity by means of a disapproving look is the recommended procedure. If a scapegoat is not available, J.P. Donleavy has suggested that one should pretend to look for a gas seepage between the floorboards. The search should be accompanied by a look of disbelief at the awful smell that has suddenly made itself known. This ruse, he suggests, will be understood by other fair-minded wind-breakers.

A web page that tells foreign learners of English about some of the ruder words in the language explains that 'a fart is the noisy and/or smelly gas which comes out of your bottom' and that a 'belch is air coming out through the mouth'. After the curious comment: 'make sure you know which end it has come from' (about which, surely, there is rarely any doubt), foreigners are told that 'in Britain, it is not good manners to fart or belch in public. If you have an accident, don't say anything – just give the person next to you a dirty look. Everyone else will then think that he or she did it.' See also *Shifting the blame*.

Painting the elevator

Bob Burton Brown's *Maledicta* article, 'Windy Words', mentions this interesting family reference to farting. It relates to the embarrassing situation that arises after you 'let a real stinker' in an elevator, thinking you are alone. Somebody then gets on at the next floor before the smell has dispersed. Professor Brown says: 'You wrinkle up your nose and say, "They must have just painted this elevator." In our family we all know what it means when one of us asks, "Who painted the elevator?"'

Pantyhose

The pantyhose joke runs: 'How can you tell when a woman is wearing pantyhose?' 'When she farts her ankles blow up!'

Pardon

Used as a synonym of 'fart'. See also *Excuse me!*

Parliamentary gas

Frank Harris relates an anecdote about a famous parliamentary fart in *My Life*. Finch-Hatton, a newly-elected member, was sitting next to Sir Robert Fowler, who rose to make a speech. While speaking, Sir Robert also perfumed the air around him with a particularly foul exhalation. Finch-Hatton edged as far away from him as he could. 'As soon as Fowler sat down,' says

Harris, 'Finch-Hatton sprang up holding his handkerchief to his nose. "Mr Speaker," he began, and was at once acknowledged by the Speaker, for it was a maiden speech, and as such was entitled to precedence by the courteous custom of the House. "I know why the Right Honourable Member from the City did not conclude his speech with a proposal. The only way to conclude such a speech appropriately would be with a motion!"'

For another anecdote about Sir Robert Fowler's smelliness, see *Crack*.

Pass gas

A common euphemism, especially in the US, for farting, though not yet recognized as such by British or American lexicographers. Somebody who has just passed gas is likely to be accused of having 'gassed us out'. Traditional American medical humour has it that anaesthesiologists 'sit on a stool all day and pass gas'. They are also referred to as 'gas-passers', something which is said to afford them great amusement. To 'pass gas' is a relatively neutral expression. Its variants include 'pass air' and 'pass wind'.

A contributor to an Internet forum reported that 'in Burbank during the '70s there was a filling station on Pass Avenue called Pass Gas.' He added: 'By the way, in Israel the main gas company is called Paz.'

Passive farting

See *Fartee*.

Peasant's fart, The

Le Pet au Vilain (The Peasant's Fart) is a French *fabliau*, of the kind that was highly popular in the thirteenth and fourteenth centuries. Susan Whitebook, Professor of Romance Languages, summarizes it as follows: 'A poor peasant had the good fortune to eat a huge roast and was suffering from indigestion as a consequence. He thought he was going to die, so Satan sent a fresh new devil with a sack in which to catch his soul. The devil was so inexperienced that he put the sack at the wrong end, and when the peasant broke wind, and hugely, the devil caught that and rushed back to hell. The sack was opened, and the foul odour filled the place. That is why French peasants no longer go to hell.'

Pedo, ergo sum

A Latin tag, meaning 'I fart, therefore I exist.' This is thought by some scholars to have inspired Descartes's variant *Cogito, ergo sum*, which is usually translated as 'I think, therefore I am.' The original version clearly has more of a claim to be a general truism. Not everybody thinks, in the way that Descartes had in mind, at least, but everybody farts.

Peppermints

In earlier times peppermint water was believed to have carminative properties, preventing wind. Modern restaurants often acknowledge this by providing an after-dinner peppermint, though most diners are probably unaware that they are being given a fart-preventer.

Perdological salutations

This phrase refers to what people say to greet or comment on their own fart. Reported examples (where the speaker is male in all cases) include 'take that!' 'good health!' 'catch that and paint it blue', 'hang your hat on that one!' 'there's a kiss for somebody!' 'there goes the elephant!' 'better hang on to that!' 'more room outside than inside!' 'must be a mouse under this chair!' 'better out than in!' Lisa Hoyman says of her father that 'when he passed gas he would afterward put on an air of deep thought and consideration, and then say, "Oh . . . that was um . . . about a C-Sharp, I think." The musical note he chose varied, though I doubt that the tone of the emission was much

different from one instance to another.' J.P. Donleavy has suggested that a cheerful 'Whoops!' by the wind-breaker may well earn him 'a little patter of clapping' from his audience.

The young Australian lady whose boyfriend always said 'the big brown bear is roaring in his cave' when he broke wind is now, as she herself was at pains to stress, her ex-boyfriend. She did not elaborate on whether it was the act or the comment to which she took objection.

Crepitators are often reduced to saluting their own achievements in this kind of way since the most they can usually expect from other people is the equivalent of a groan (but see *Friendly comments*). The expression 'butt sneeze', used by some American students to describe an anal emission, reminds us that the situation is quite different when someone sneezes. For some reason a sneeze usually inspires a 'bless you!' from even hardened atheists who happen to be present, even though a sneeze, like a fart, is merely an involuntary, natural human noise.

In his article 'Rearing' (made available on the Internet) Tim Rogers says that he 'thought for a moment about saying "bless you"' when his future mother-in-law broke wind. Rogers is joking as usual, but there is surely no reason why 'bless you', or perhaps 'good health', could not be extended to farting. The latter act, after all, merely perfumes the air for a moment or two or provides mild amusement by its sound. It deserves a greeting. A sneeze is unpleasant and likely to pass on contagious germs. It is the sneezer, not the farter, who merits our disapproval.

Perdology

Perdology means 'the scientific study of farts'. The word was a neologism invented by Peter Furze, based on the Greek verb *perdein* 'to break wind'. Peter also used the word 'perdological' to mean 'pertaining to farts'.

Pet

This is the normal word for 'fart' in French. It derives from Latin *peditus*, later *pettus*, as does Italian *peto*. *Pet* was briefly borrowed into English in the sixteenth century, as in Barclay's *Eclogues* (1515): 'Though all their cunning scantly be worth a pet.' At the time the English language was fairly rich in 'fart' words, and had no real need of such foreign imports. The word is nevertheless said to be used by some French-Canadians who refer very confusingly to 'farting' as 'petting'. One wonders how young Canadians describe what they do with their girlfriends when the opportunity arises.

Pétain

This famous French surname almost certainly indicates an ancestor who was known for his remarkable farting. Similar last names are Pétard, Pethard, Peton, Petot, Petter, Pettour. See also *Christmas entertainment*.

Peterau

French for 'a small fart'. See also *Squib*.

Le Pétomane

Le Pétomane, the man who took Paris by storm between 1892 and 1900 with his unique farting act, was Joseph Pujol (1857–1945), born in Marseilles. (*Pétomane* is a non-existent French word, roughly equivalent to 'fartomaniac'.) During his act at Le Moulin Rouge, Pujol would announce before farting, 'this is a little girl,' or 'this is the mother-in-law,' 'this is the bride on her wedding night' (a very quiet fart) and 'this is her the morning after' (very loud). He could produce sounds ranging from a dressmaker tearing calico to that of cannon being fired or thunder rumbling. He could imitate the sounds of various animals and birds. After sticking a rubber tube into his anus he would smoke a cigarette. By adding a little flute to the end of the tube he would then play tunes, such as '*Au Clair de la Lune*'. He was a huge commercial success, taking far more at the box-office, for example, than Sarah Bernhardt, then at the height of her fame.

The English translation of Pujol's biography, by Jean Nohain and F. Caradec, was published by Sphere Books in 1971. This relates that as a boy, when bathing in the sea, Pujol had discovered that he could absorb water through his anus, then eject it at will. Later he found that he could also stop breathing through his nose and mouth and take in air in the same way. By contracting his muscles he was then able to modulate the sound as the air was expelled, creating a 'fart fantasia'. Since the air he was expelling had not been contaminated with the usual intestinal gases, there was no smell. Nor was there any methane in his farts, which was probably just as well. It was his custom to end his act by blowing out the gas-lights along the front of the stage. Had his farts contained methane he would have become a kind of anal flame-thrower.

Pujol allowed himself to be examined under laboratory conditions by various doctors. They certified that in his case 'the intestine plays the role of the chest in storing air and the anal sphincter that of the vocal chords, the throat and the mouth. He uses his abdominal cavity like a bellows, the anterior and posterior walls being the two valves, the rectum the pipe.' Pujol's was a very rare case, but not unique: Montaigne had mentioned similar men in the sixteenth century.

Pujol eventually quarrelled with the management of Le Moulin Rouge and left. A woman, Angèle Thiebeau, replaced him with a similar act, but Pujol took her to court and was able to prove that she was a phoney farter, working with a pair of bellows under her skirt. He himself lived happily in his retirement with his large family, continuing to amuse his friends and relatives with his fart-based entertainments.

Phantom farter

A way of referring to the unknown person in a group who is making a personal aromatic contribution to the proceedings, while managing to conceal his or her identity.

Phewy

An emission of gas, often silent, that makes itself known by its rank smell.

Physagogue

Derived from Greek words meaning 'flatulence' and 'drawing forth'. *The Oxford English Dictionary* defines it as 'expelling flatus'. The word was also occasionally used in the nineteenth century for a medicine having this effect.

Pinch-fart

Thomas Nash uses this expression in his *Pierce Pennilesse* (1592), referring to 'my pinch-fart penny-father'. It is clear that he means 'miserly', since misers were variously known at the time as pinch-bellies, pinch-crusts, pinch-guts, pinch-pennies. They were also called pinch-fists, perhaps a synonym for pinch-farts (see *Fyst*). 'Pinch' had not yet acquired its slang meaning of 'steal' and is probably to be interpreted as 'squeeze'. The term suggests a man who is mean enough to want to keep everything to himself, even his farts.

Poop

This is used as a slang word for 'excrement', but it has long had the alternative meaning 'fart'. Bailey's *Universal Etymological English Dictionary* (1751) glosses the verb 'poop' as 'to break wind backwards softly'. A few years earlier (1744) a nursery rhyme was published which read:

> Little Robin Redbreast
> Sitting on a pole
> Niddle, Noddle
> Went his head
> And poop went his hole.

Later editors of nursery rhymes invariably changed the last line, since 'poop', like other 'fart' words, was subsequently banished from polite conversation. It nevertheless remained in use: Eric Partridge included it in his *Dictionary of Slang* (1937), still with the meaning 'a breaking of wind'. In many contemporary American families, 'poop' is the 'fart' word used to and by the children. It has the occasional variants 'poopie' and 'poops'. 'Poopfume' is sometimes used as a humorous variant of 'perfume', with reference to the strong smell of an emission.

A contributor to an Internet forum mentioned that in southern California there was once a (very good) Thai restaurant called the Poo-Ping Palace.

Poot
· · · · ·

An American slang word for 'fart'. Donald M. Lance reports from Missouri that this was 'our family word for breaking wind' – obviously onomatopoeic in origin. It is also probably influenced by childish words for excrement, such as 'poo' and 'poop'. The Lance family version of a well-known rhyme was:

> Beans, beans, the musical fruit;
> The more you eat, the more you poot.

See also *Toot*.

Pop off
· · · · · · · ·

'Pop, pop off, pop a whiff, popping' and the like are widely reported (Britain, America, Australia) as mainly childish references to farting. 'Popper' and 'multipopper' are used as nouns. Professor Sheila Embleton has suggested that there is 'a fairly obvious origin in baby-talk'. She has heard references to 'poppy botties', leading to phrases like 'my botty popped'. Professor Embleton adds: 'I've never heard these expressions except where kids are involved in the conversation.'

Pregnant farts

It is well known that women in the later stages of pregnancy are likely to fart audibly, although they would normally be able to control such matters. This can come as a shock to young husbands, who find it difficult to associate their loved ones with something normally restricted to the world of male vulgarity. John Updike comments on the situation in *Rabbit is Rich*, saying that 'What Nelson can't stand about Pru, she farts.' (Pru is seven months pregnant.) Updike helpfully adds: 'Now Pru farts because of some way the baby is displacing her insides.'

Pretentious fart

There is a curious conversation in *The Buddha of Suburbia*, by Hanif Kureishi. 'Pretentious,' says one speaker. 'Yes,' is the reply, 'the sound of one buttock farting.' The reference is perhaps to the farting sound made as a buttock is lifted from a chair, but why this should be considered pretentious is a mystery.

Proletarian farts

'A proletarian fart is greater music than a bourgeois song,' he said, and she grimaced and said, 'You wish.'

Louis de Bernières, *Captain Corelli's Mandolin*

Proverbial farts

Farts are not frequently mentioned in English proverbial sayings – not in those that have survived, at least. John Heywood's collection of *Proverbs and Epigrams*, published in 1562, includes: 'I shall get a fart of a dead man as soon as a farthing of him.' A pun involving 'farting' and 'farthing' may have been intended. He also quotes: 'He that is afraid of every fart must go far to piss.' John Ray's proverb collection of 1670 has: 'It's good farting before one's own fire'; 'As lazy as the tinker who laid down his budget [bag] to fart'; 'As free as a dead horse is of farts.'

Almost proverbial in modern times is the remark that a schoolboy is likely to make if someone accuses him of having broken wind: 'A dog smells his own shit first.' From America comes report of a saying: 'A farting horse will never tire. That's the type of man to hire.' Presumably it is the 'never tiring' that is being commended, not the 'farting'.

Prump

A synonym for 'fart' listed in Orton and Halliday's *Survey of English Dialects* (Northern counties). It is not in *The Oxford English Dictionary*. Presumably the word imitates the sound of a fart.

Puff

Eric Partridge says in his *Dictionary of Historical Slang* that 'puff' became a euphemism for 'fart' in the late nineteenth and early twentieth centuries. ('I hope all those beans we ate for supper don't make us puff all night.') The allusion was to a puff of wind or to smoking a cigarette or cigar. As far as the latter is concerned, Tiparillo, the brand name of a cigar, has been used as a euphemism for a fart, the allusion no doubt being to its smell.

Oddly, in the sixteenth century, there had been a half-hearted attempt to use the word 'fart' to describe the ball of light pastry known as a 'puff'. This was in imitation of French. For the link between puff-ball fungi and 'fart' see also *Wolf fart*.

Pull my finger

Lisa Hoyman writes: 'When Dad felt the need to pass gas, he would sometimes say to the nearest person (preferably one of his offspring), "Pull my finger, would you?" Of course, as the finger was pulled the gas was passed.'

This joke, which young children (as well as Beavis and Butt-Head) usually enjoy greatly, was mentioned in the 1991 film *Another You*. Gene Wilder, playing the role of a compulsive liar, related that he was once in an English lift with a certain Lady Tushingham, who asked him to pull her finger. When he did so the lift was filled with an appalling aroma. Unfortunately, said Wilder, at that moment Lord Tushingham decided to light his cigar. He – Wilder – was saved from the wreckage of the subsequent explosion by his friend (Richard Pryor).

Punctuating a conversation

In *A Cack-Handed War*, Edward Blishen writes: 'Take a sack off his lorry, and quick as one of the farts with which he punctuated his conversations he'd seat himself upon it.' This interesting idea could be expanded, with different kinds of fart performing the functions of comma, full stop, question mark, and so on. An Internet posting which gives names to various emissions mentions the Exclamation Fart.

Pursiness

A word used in the seventeenth century to refer to flatulence. A text of 1607 says: 'As he is outwardly full of unsound fatness, so he is inwardly stuffed with much glut and pursiness.'

Putt

Used for 'fart' by, for example, Sylvia Branzei in *Grossology*. It was no doubt suggested by the sound of certain farts, or by similar words such as 'poot'. 'Putt-putt' and 'putz' also occur, the latter accidentally resembling the Yiddish word for 'penis', used of an obnoxious person. The rare use of 'punt' for 'fart' may also derive from 'putt'.

Queef

A euphemism for 'fart'. See also *Beef*.

Queries

In *Mating*, Norman Rush writes: 'There are going to be incidents of flatus and we are going to ignore them and refer to them as queries.' This is in the context of a woman giving a man a back massage. 'The first time I had sensed I'd gotten him deeply relaxed a fart had escaped him. He was horrified and got tense.'

Rabbit's fart

The French refer to this when they say *ça ne vaut pas un pet de lapin*, literally 'it's not worth a rabbit's fart.' A more colloquial translation would be 'it's worth damn all.' See also *Gunshots*.

Raising a buttock

Many people who are able to fart silently give themselves away to anyone who is watching because they raise a buttock to let the gas escape. The result may be what is known as a 'one-cheek sneak'. Those who intend to fart loudly, of course, may raise a buttock in a similar way. A joke that circulates in medical circles concerns an elderly man admitted to a nursing home. Soon after his arrival a nurse sees him lolling over to the left in his chair. She props a pillow under that side to stop him hurting himself. Later she sees him leaning over to the right, so she puts a pillow there as well. Later still she sees him apparently falling forward, so she fixes him up with a vest restraint. That evening the man's relatives come to see him and ask how he is getting on. 'The nurse is real nice,' he tells them, 'but she sure doesn't like you to fart around here.'

Henry Miller comments on this same phenomenon in *Tropic of Cancer*: 'By way of showing us what a nude ought to be like he hauls out a huge canvas which he had recently completed. It was a picture of *her*, a splendid piece of vengeance inspired by a guilty conscience. The most prominent thing was her buttocks, which were lopsided and full of scabs; she seemed slightly to have raised her ass from the sofa, as if to let a loud fart.' Miller missed a golden opportunity to describe this particular painting as 'arty-farty'.

Raspberry

This derives from 'raspberry tart', rhyming slang for 'fart', but the word seems to be used only of the disapproving sound which imitates a fart, made by sticking the tongue out and blowing. An American term for this oral imitation of a sputtering fart is 'Bronx cheer'. From the idea of expressing disapproval, 'raspberry' took on the meaning of a 'reprimand', as when

P.G. Wodehouse writes, in *The Inimitable Jeeves*: 'He was given the respectful raspberry by Jeeves, and told to try again about three hours later.'

Rats

Dann Lennard reports from Australia that male colleagues who suspect someone of farting are likely to ask: 'Did a rat crawl up your arse and die?' A similar enquiry was mentioned by an American student in 1997: 'What crawled up in you and died?'

Rattler

A fart which is theoretically loud enough to rattle nearby cups and saucers.

Rax

'He's raxing again' for 'he's farting again' is quoted in Orton and Halliday's *Survey of English Dialects* (Northern counties). The basic meaning of 'rax' seems to be 'stretch, strain', which in turn conjures up an image of contorted features and a raised buttock.

Record-breaking farts

The *Guinness Book of Records* makes no mention of record-breaking farts or farters. Perhaps it should do so. In *Tropic of Cancer*, Henry Miller mentions a man named Kroa, 'who belched like a pig and always let off a loud fart when he sat down to table. He could fart thirteen times in succession, they informed me. He held the record.' This is amongst the assistant teachers in a school. Sylvia Branzei, in *Grossology*, says that a man from Minneapolis farted 141 times in a 24-hour period, though that figure is based on his own count. Record-breaking farting events would need independent adjudicators to have any recognized validity.

Redneck definition

The American Jeff Foxworthy is known for his series of one-liners on the theme: 'You're a redneck if . . .' Typical continuations are: 'you go to the family reunion to meet women'; 'you own a home that is mobile and 14 cars that aren't'; 'you've ever been accused of lying through your tooth'. He also has one that states: 'You're a redneck if your dog passes gas and you claim it.'

Relationship indicator

There are those who say that when a man is willing to break wind in the presence of a woman, it is a reassuring sign that their relationship is firmly established. If the couple are not married already, they are ready to tie the knot. Many women, however, do not subscribe to the idea that admitting a man to

their bed or exchanging wedding vows with him automatically gives him the right to fart at will. The 'Women of Greater Atlanta Online Magazine' once published a letter from 'Wendy' which probably represents the views of many wives: 'Dear Vikki, is there help for me? I've been married for six years now and although I love my husband to death, there is one thing that really ticks me off. Why is it that you date a guy for a year and he's adoring and loving and wonderful. Then you marry him and he feels the need to pass gas and burp ALL THE TIME.' Vikki's reply in this case was not very helpful: 'Dear Wendy, there is nothing I can do. It is a defective gene in all men.'

Perhaps Vikki could have advised Wendy to reply in kind. The same experts say that if a woman feels free to pass gas in the presence of the man, their relationship is especially healthy. Many couples do not reach this stage of openness with one another. They feel compelled to bottle up their gas, which may in turn make them momentarily irritable. Young people in the early stages of a relationship, observing the frown which suddenly contorts a partner's face, should not automatically assume that they have done something to offend. The frown may merely reflect the discomfort caused by perdological repression.

In *Mating*, by Norman Rush, a couple who live together gradually come to terms with the problem of flatulence. 'In our first days together we had individually found reasons to go outside for a minute, especially after we'd gone to bed, to avoid the antiromance of it all. But that got to be too much. We developed a fairly decent modus, I thought. He might say, when I was the author, *Also sprach Zarathustra* [thus spake Zarathustra, a reference to the founder of Zoroastrianism] or Ah, a report from the interior, as though he were an ambassador or proconsul. These and some other coinages evolved as we became more comfortable with each other. This condition does have to be worked through between lovers. I know of a marriage where the first hairline crack that led to a full collapse appeared when the husband claimed that flatulence was only a problem when he did the cooking.'

Remembrance of Farts Past

This is the name of a web site which has a curiosity value, apart from its successful punning title. The musician 'Evil Bob' offers visitors a music module, of which he says: 'It is a piece of music which I composed some time ago on the *Amiga* using the *OctaMED* sequencer. It is notable because it is probably the first (and only) through-composed composition in western music history which uses digitized farts as primary source material. These farts were originally "performed" by my buddy D.G. Thanks to his tireless dedication to capturing his profane and nasty little bodily noises for the enrichment of others, I was provided with an excellent musical ensemble.'

Representing the sound of a fart

Capturing the sound of a fart in print faces authors with a considerable challenge. 'Pfpt' is used for a disappointing fart sound by Douglas Adams and John Lloyd, in *The Meaning of Liff*. Sylvia Branzei, in *Grossology*, favours 'flub, flubba, fwwwp,' though she also mentions the fart noises 'fwwt', 'put-put-put', 'pwwwbbbb' and the 'flubba-flub'. In *Ulysses*, at the end of the 'Sirens' episode, James Joyce gives us his idea of a fart sound – 'Karaaaaaaa . . . Pprrpffrrppfff'.

Rhubarb

According to a traditional English saying:

> Rhubarb crumble makes you rumble
> Rhubarb tart makes you fart.

As it happens, 'rumble' is in occasional use as a euphemism for 'fart'.

Rift

A synonym for 'fart' used in some dialects of northern England. The word appears to suggest a splitting, or gaping open, but 'rift' in that sense is from Old Norse *ripta*, whereas the 'rift' that means fart is from Old Norse *ropi*. The latter word normally refers to belching, but its meaning has been expanded to include a downward breaking of wind.

Rip
····

This normally occurs in the phrase 'let one rip', to break wind loudly, but 'rip one', 'rip one off' and 'rip your pants' are sometimes used with a similar meaning. Once an emission has been ripped off it is described as a 'ripper'. The headline on the front page of the London *Times* (21 March 1997) was: 'Major lets rip at Blair and Ashdown.' The opening sentence of the article explained that John Major had 'unleashed a venomous assault on Tony Blair and Paddy Ashdown', a statement which was still rather ambiguous, but the assault seems to have been only a verbal one.

Room-clearer
················

A name given to a fart that has an especially bad smell.

Rosepetal
···········

A euphemism for 'fart'. See *Feminine toots*. 'Drop a rose' is also a slang way of referring to breaking wind. There is presumably a connection with 'rosebud', an American slang term for the anus. Another related term is used by Hal J. Daniel III, at the beginning of his poem 'Whew, Ah':

> Have you ever
> slept with a sweet one
> only to feel
> a big one
> about to be blown
> out your rosette?

Rotten eggs

An evil-smelling fart is often compared to rotten eggs, but one should not necessarily jump to conclusions when that odour makes itself apparent. Dame Edna Everage, in *My Gorgeous Life*, writes: 'We at last reached New Zealand's famous volcanic zone. Even as we approached, the air started to smell of rotten eggs. Knowing Madge as well as I did, I instinctively wound down the window, only to realize that that horrid sulphurous odour came from without.'

Rouser

A slang reference to a noisy emission of gas.

Rush around like a fart along a curtain rod

This translates the German idiom: *hin und her sausen* [or *rasen*] *wie ein Furz auf der Gardinenstange*. A sense of agitation was formerly conveyed in English by the slang expressions 'rush around like a fart in a bottle', and 'in and out like a fart in a colander'.

Sauna farts

J.P. Donleavy, in *The Unexpurgated Code*, says that farting in a sauna 'can occasion the dreadful stifling phenomenon of the baked fart'.

SBD

An American acronymic euphemism for a fart, mentioned by Neaman and Silver in *A Dictionary of Euphemisms*. The letters stand for 'silent but dangerous (or deadly)'. In medical circles an SBD is sometimes called a 'tacit fart'. A survey carried out in February 1997 amongst American students revealed that the improved variant 'silent but violent' is also now in use. Others refer to a 'silent killer' or 'stealth bomber'. All of these expressions reflect the common belief that silent farts smell worse than loud ones. It is said, however, that any potentially loud fart can be toned down if the farter can manage to spread the cheeks of his buttocks. Alternatively, he should hastily sit on a well-cushioned chair.

Scape

To 'let a scape' was a common euphemism for 'fart' in the sixteenth and seventeenth centuries. It derived from 'escape', and is sometimes found in that form. A text of 1599, for instance, relates that a young man 'meeting Alice Goodridge in a coppice did let an escape', behaviour which apparently did not amuse Alice in the least. She interpreted the fart as 'done in her contempt' and departed in a huff, presumably holding her nose.

An earlier writer made an interesting link between farting and laughing: 'I for my part, through laughter, had almost let go a scape, as Priapus did.' Another complained of those who used 'the language of dissimulation', referring to a scape as a 'cough'. In this instance the commentator seems not to have noticed that he was himself dissimulating, using 'scape' for 'fart'.

Scotch Warming-Pan

A breaking of wind in bed, with an unkind allusion to the supposed meanness of the Scots and their not wishing to pay for hot water to be used in a warming-pan.

Self-flatulation

A concept dreamed up by Brad Whittington, who maintains a web site devoted to *Almost Great Men In Church History*. He remarks that 'during the Middle Ages, asceticism increased as a means to piety largely due to the efforts of St Smyth, who pioneered self-flatulation. This practice gained wider acceptance in its modified form, self-flagellation.' 'Self-flatulation' certainly manages to imply that one can mortify oneself by sniffing one's farts, but for many men this practice is far too pleasurable to be considered a mortification.

Sent away to fart

If you are told in French to 'eff off, bugger off', you are probably being told, literally, to go away and fart. 'He told me to clear off' in colloquial French is *il m'a envoyé péter*.

Shakespeare and farting

The nearest Shakespeare comes to using the word 'fart' is in *The Merry Wives of Windsor*, where Mistress Quickly is talking to Falstaff about Mistress Page: 'she's as fartuous a civil modest wife, and one, I tell you, that will not miss you morning nor evening prayer, as any is in Windsor.' 'Fartuous' here is Mistress Quickly's form of 'virtuous'.

Elsewhere in the plays there are various allusions to farting. When Ophelia tells her father, for example, that Hamlet has made many 'tenders' of his affection to her, her father mocks her for taking Hamlet's remarks seriously: 'you have ta'en these tenders for true pay, which are not sterling. Tender yourself more dearly; or – not to crack the wind of the poor phrase, running it thus – you'll tender me a fool.' 'Crack' was already in use at this time as a synonym for 'fart', and 'crack the wind' would have pleased the groundlings. *Hamlet* also has the 'hoist with his own petard' remark, referring to being blown up by one's own bomb, or caught in one's own trap. The saying is sometimes applied to a person who is obliged to smell his own fart. This is apt, since 'petard' – a small explosive device for blowing in doors – derives ultimately from Latin *pedere* 'to fart'.

In *Othello*, the clown has a conversation with the musicians in Act III, and asks: 'Are these, I pray you, wind-instruments?' He is told that they are. 'Thereby hangs a tail,' says the clown. 'Whereby hangs a tale, sir?' asks the first musician. 'Marry, sir,' says the clown, 'by many a wind-instrument that I know.' An Elizabethan audience would immediately have picked up the allusion to the 'tail', or 'penis', being close to the anal 'wind-instrument'.

Some of Shakespeare's references to 'scapes' allow a farty interpretation, and several 'breaking wind' references occur.

The Comedy of Errors has Dromio of Ephesus saying: 'A man may break a word with you, sir, and words are but wind, ay, and break it in your face, so he break it not behind.' In *Timon of Athens*, Alcibiades tells the senators 'now breathless wrong shall sit and pant in your great chairs of ease, and pursy insolence shall break his wind with fear and horrid flight.' In *King Henry IV, Part I*, when Falstaff says 'I shall break my wind,' he is theoretically saying that he will be breathless, but the double-meaning is intended.

There is a more interesting passage in this same play where the planet itself is likened to someone suffering from wind. Hotspur is scornfully dismissing the portents that supposedly marked Glendower's birth: 'Diseased nature oftentimes breaks forth in strange eruptions; oft the teeming earth is with a kind of colic pinch'd and vex'd by the imprisoning of unruly wind within her womb; which, for enlargement striving shakes the old beldam earth and topples down steeples and moss-grown towers.'

Although Shakespeare is often bawdy, he is restrained in his references to flatulence. Perhaps he knew that his actors would provide a fart or two during performances, whether his text called for them or not. As the memoirs of many actors make clear, farting on stage is very much part of Thespian tradition. See also *Crab*.

Shifting the blame
....

As mentioned previously (see *Blaming the dog*), it is accepted practice when a bad smell fills the room to blame the nearest dog if one happens to be available. If a 'scape-dog', so to speak, is not available the blame should be shifted elsewhere. While the O.J. Simpson trial was in progress, it became briefly fashionable amongst some Americans to announce that 'OJ did it!' A more realistic side-stepping is possible when the gas-passer is dining in a chic restaurant: he simply blames a passing waiter for an embarrassing noise or smell. The waiter is usually happy to accept responsibility if he thinks that a large tip will come his way. If the client is known to be mean, or is disliked for other reasons, he may not be so obliging. 'Waiter, stop that!' said one haughty lady when she inadvertently broke wind loudly. 'Certainly, madam,' replied the waiter, 'which way did it go?'

Martial (*Book IV, Epigram LXXX*), long ago mentioned another way of shifting the blame. 'Your Bassa, Fabulius, has always a child at her side, calling it her darling and her plaything; and yet – more wonder – she does not care for children. What is the reason then? Bassa is apt to fart.'

Similes

Farting similes seem to be surprisingly rare. 'Fart like a heavy horse' has been recorded, but one would have expected a series of phrases beginning 'fart like a . . .' Other objects or ideas are more commonly compared to farts: 'like a fart in a wind tunnel', etc. The Canadian novelist Guy Vanderhaeghe, in his novel *The Englishman's Boy*, writes: 'My letter isn't righteous or impolite, it simply treats what happened at the party as if it hadn't, like a fart at a formal dinner. Not a mention.'

Singing hymns

This was the phrase used by an American informant who was asked by the editors of the *American Dictionary of Regional English* how he referred to 'breaking wind from the bowels'.

Sit on an elephant

An American expression referring to a threatened fart, as in 'I'm sitting on an elephant.' This is linked to the idea of the elephant's trumpeting. Some speakers say instead that there is 'an elephant on my back'.

Slider

'Sliders' are farts that unobtrusively 'slide out'. A particularly successful fart of this kind is now sometimes called an 'easy slider'. 'Slider' seems to have been introduced to the American public in this sense by the *Merck Manual of Diagnosis and Therapy*, a popular and authoritative medical text. The word is more commonly associated with a particular kind of pitch in baseball.

Smell

A child's word for a fart, used in the phrase 'to let a smell (or smelly)'. 'Who's smelling?' can also be used for 'Who's farted?'

Smell the fart acting

Modern actors' slang for a technique that is used when a moment is needed to remember a line or consult an idiot-board. The actor adopts a slightly puzzled look and appears to be gently sniffing the air as he looks around him.

Smoking

A person who is thought to be responsible for the foul smell that has suddenly made its presence felt is likely to be told, 'Stop smoking!' or 'This is a no-smoking area!' It has also been suggested that 'Thank you for not smoking' signs should alternate in public establishments with others saying 'Thank you for not farting.'

The connection between the smell of stale tobacco and a fart has long been established. There is an interesting dialogue in *The Provok'd Wife*, by Sir John Vanbrugh, between Lady Brute and her niece. The pipe that Sir John Brute is smoking in their presence causes Belinda, the niece, to say that she would dislike her husband 'if he smoked tobacco'. Her aunt replies: 'Why, that, many times, takes off worse smells.' 'Then he must smell very ill indeed,' says Belinda. 'So some men will,' says Lady Brute, 'to keep their wives from coming near them.'

A slang dictionary published in 1700 defined the noun 'funk' as 'tobacco smoke, also a strong smell or stink'. John Brockett's *Glossary of North Country Words*, which appeared in various editions in the 1820s, also says that 'funk' is 'to smoke, or rather to cause an offensive smell'.

Snappers

In parts of the USA 'snappers' are beans, and by extension, the farts that come after the beans have been eaten.

Sneaky one

A reference to a fart that has quietly been contributed to the proceedings without anyone noticing.

Sniffle

A family euphemism for 'fart', noun and verb, reported by Professor Bob Burton Brown.

Solemn considerations

The need to break wind can occur at any time, including occasions when it is the last thing someone would wish to do. There is the case of the devout believer, for example, who is in the middle of praying but cannot prevent an emission of gas. This could be deeply distressful to the person concerned, as if it were an unwitting blasphemous act. Advice on the matter is needed, especially for those who devote their lives to their religion.

This is therefore one of the subjects discussed in depth by Project Genesis, the Jewish Learning Network, which is accessible on the Internet. There is an interesting historical summary of the views of eminent authorities, showing how their thoughts on the matter have modified slightly since the seventeenth century. Sensible consideration has been given to whether a person is praying publicly or privately, whether the flatulation is audible or inaudible, and so on. The modern view appears to be: 'If you were in the midst of prayer and flatulated, you should wait until the strong smell has passed by and then continue praying.'

Sounding off

'Sounding' and 'sounding off' are occasional American military euphemisms for farting, presumably derived from the practice of counting the cadence while marching. However, someone who is making his opinions known in a vigorous manner is also said to be 'sounding off'. Breaking wind loudly in company could perhaps be considered a way of expressing an opinion.

Southern talk

In *You All Spoken Here*, Roy Wilder lists a number of colloquial flatulent expressions used in the southern states of America. 'He's so lazy he stops plowin' to fart' speaks for itself. A 'strut fart' is a person highly conscious of his own importance. To say that someone 'had a fartin' spell' means that he displayed bad temper. Amongst the oilmen someone who is considered to be a windbag would be said to be 'passin' gas faster'n he can cap it'. In the farmyards a 'cackling fart' is an egg. Strong coffee is referred to in the saying: 'as strong as horse piss with the foam farted off'.

How to Talk Dirty Like Grandpa, by Tom Ladwig, adds two further sayings. 'I'm dryer than a popcorn fart' indicates that the speaker is badly in need of a drink. 'It must be coming up your shirttail' is glossed as 'I don't smell what you smell'.

Spam

This processed meat is occasionally mentioned as a rival to beans in its fart-producing qualities. There is even a variant of the 'musical fruit' rhyme (see *Toot*) which runs:

> Spam, spam, the magical food,
> The more you eat, the more you're crude.

Spanish farts

'To fart' in Spanish is *tirarse un pedo* or *echarse un pedo*. The -*arse* that appears in these expressions is a linguistic coincidence; there is no connection with the English word. *Soltar el preso*, a slang expression used in Spanish for an eructation, would aptly describe a fart. It translates literally as 'unloose/untie the prisoner'.

Spit it out

A contemporary American slang term for the verb 'fart'.

Spoonerism

'He was a real fart smeller – uh, I mean, a real smart feller.'

Spoot

A rare American variant of 'toot'.

Squeaking

Beavis and Butt-Head refer to passing gas as 'squeaking a breeze'. 'Are you sitting in a squeaking chair?' is a sarcastic way of making it clear that someone's gas emissions have been noticed. 'This chair squeaks' may alternatively be offered as a lame excuse by the flatulator himself. The squeaking is occasionally blamed on a mouse, as when Mark Twain refers in 1601 to a young girl tickling her maidenhood 'with many a mousie-squeak'.

Squeezer

A trumpet-like breaking of wind, caused by squeezing the buttocks together.

Squib

Randle Cotgrave's *English French Dictionary*, published in 1611, glosses *peterau* as 'a little fart, or squib'. Urquhart was later to rely heavily on this dictionary for his translation of Rabelais. As one might expect, therefore, Urquhart writes at one point: 'Often-times thinking to let a squib, they did all-to-besquatter themselves.' The firework known as a squib had come into use in the early sixteenth century. Its hissing sound, followed by a small explosion, made it highly suitable to be compared with a fart. Rather later came the phrase 'damp squib', which takes on a new meaning in this context.

Stewart

A slang expression for 'fart'. See *Comic Relief*.

Stinker

A fairly common way of referring to a fart that perhaps goes unnoticed to the ear, but makes itself known to the noses of those present. 'Stink' and 'stinkie' are variants.

Stink glands

There are many animals which make use of anal stink glands as a defence mechanism. They cannot be said to be farting in the face of the enemy,

since they are not actually expelling flatus. The skunk or polecat is well known for the stink it is able to produce; the badger defends itself in a similar way.

'Summoner's Tale, The'

This is another of Chaucer's *Canterbury Tales* (see also 'Miller's Tale, The'). Its theme is how to divide the sound and the smell of a fart equally between thirteen monks.

Taking exception

There are occasions when a person can be seriously upset by someone else breaking wind. In December, 1996, police responded to a 911 (emergency) call in Janesville, Wisconsin, to find a man and his wife engaged in a full-scale battle. The domestic disturbance had begun, explained the wife, because the husband had farted at an inappropriate moment. He had done it, she said, when they had been tucking their son into bed.

There are countless wives who object to their husband's farting habits, classing such behaviour as insulting to themselves. In extreme cases it contributes to the ending of the marriage – see *Grounds for divorce*.

Talk German

One of the many slang expressions for 'fart'.

Teachers

'If you see a young character who teaches or has taught, you know you're up against some sort of dreary little fart right away. There are no exceptions to this. Teaching is the American for second-rate.'

Wilfrid Sheed, *The Critic*

Technological achievements

An American playing golf with a Japanese businessman was surprised to see his opponent talking to his thumb. The Japanese saw his enquiring look and explained: 'It's modern micro-technology. I have a tiny microphone in my thumb, and I'm just recording a message.' Later during the round the American made a noise which sounded suspiciously like a crackerjack fart. The Japanese businessman looked at him with a raised eyebrow. 'Sorry,' said the American, 'I was just receiving a fax.'

Tee off

Another slang expression for 'fart', not necessarily confined to golfers. The 'tee' reference is probably to the initial letter of 'toot'.

Texan astonishment

It is reported that Texans have their own way of expressing astonishment. Where an Englishman might say 'I've seen a lot of things in my time, but that takes the biscuit', the Texan remarks: 'I've seen a goat-roping, a fat stock show, and a duck fart under water, but if that don't beat any damn thing I've EVER seen!'

There's a smell of gunfire

This was a comment formerly made by British soldiers when it became apparent that one of their number had farted.

Thumper

A synonym for 'fart' recorded in a survey conducted for the *Dictionary of American Regional English*. There is some evidence that 'thump' and 'thumper' were used of farting and farters in the 16th century. A play text of 1537, for instance, equates 'trumpers' with 'thumpers'.

Thunder

'Thunder' is sometimes used to refer to the sound of a rectal rampage, as in 'roll of thunder', reported by an American student, February 1977. 'Chocolate thunder', 'pocket thunder' and 'under thunder' also occur. The word is also used in combination, as when Mark Twain, in his *1601*, refers to an emission of gas as a 'thundergust'. An Australian slang term for male underpants, referring to their association with explosive flatulence, is 'thunderbags'.

'Thunder-mug' has been used to describe a chamber-pot, and the 'thunder' reference occurs again in 'thunderbox', a colloquial allusion to a toilet bowl. A character in Evelyn Waugh's *Men at Arms* says: '"If you must know, it's my thunderbox." He dragged out the treasure, a brass-bound, oak cube. On the inside of the lid was a plaque bearing the embossed title Connolly's Chemical Closet.'

Tom Tart

One of the rhyming slang expressions that has been used in the past for 'fart'. Others include 'beef-heart' ('bee-fart'), 'bullock's heart', 'heart and dart'. Apart from alliterative considerations, 'Tom' was probably chosen for 'Tom Tart' because of the name's rhyming-slang association with a 'Tom Tit', or 'shit'.

Toot

Bill King, writing from Arizona, says: 'My daughter uses "toot" for fart, as in:

Beans, beans, the musical fruit.
The more you eat, the more you toot.'

Charles Boewe mentions a slightly different version of the same rhyme, and reports that 'formerly, when a certain leguminous vegetable appeared on the menu in the dining halls at Yale University, it was met with the chant:

Beans, beans, the musical fruit,
The more you eat 'em the louder you toot.

Other sources say this rhyme continues:

The more you toot, the better you feel,
Beans, beans, at every meal.

Bill King, however, maintains that the original version is:

Beans, beans, good for the heart.
The more you eat, the more you fart.
The more you fart, the more you eat.
Let's have beans, every week.

Amongst many American schoolchildren, 'Who tooted?' would be the normal enquiry if a bad smell made it obvious that someone had offended. In some families where 'toot' is the verb, the noun form is 'tooter' or 'tootle'. Given the associations of 'toot' with the sound of wind instruments, car horns, and the like, it is a logical word to use in this context and is fairly widespread in North America. In British slang the word tends to refer to the inhalation of a drug, or the drug itself, and does not seem to be used of farting.

Torpedo

A way of referring to a violent fart released under water.

Touch bone and whistle

An American juvenile euphemism for a fart. Neaman and Silver, in their *Dictionary of Euphemisms*, suggest that it probably came about because a child who broke wind could be pinched by the others until he or she had touched a bone and whistled. An alternative version of this game involves touching a doorknob.

Toxic bum
....

A reference to a farter, reported from Australia. 'Toxic bott' was used with a similar meaning in the same family. With learned words like 'toxic' mixed in with the baby talk to which she was exposed, it is not surprising that the informant grew up to become a scientist.

Trump
....

'To trump' has been in use as a synonym for 'break wind' since the fifteenth century. Literary references to the noun 'trump' in this sense are found only at the beginning of the twentieth century, but there is no reason to suppose that it was not used earlier in speech. There is evidence that it continues to be used regionally, especially in the Midlands and the north of England. Robert Marsden, for example, originally from Nottingham, reports that 'trump' was the normal word for 'fart' in his own family circle. In a BBC television programme, shown in March 1997, Caroline Aherne in her role as the chat-show hostess Mrs Merton asked actress Joanna Lumley 'Have you just trumped?' The reaction of the audience proved that the majority of them understood what was meant, though an audience from the south of England would probably have missed the allusion.

Theoretically, 'trump' should be used of an emission which has a trumpet-like sound, or which is loud enough to attract attention to itself. Curiously, there is no evidence that 'trumpet' – etymologically 'a small trump' – has ever been used with reference to farting, though the expression 'blow one's own trumpet' would take on a new meaning if this were the case. Persistent offenders have been known as 'trumpers', but not 'trumpeters'. The early nineteenth-century expression 'he would make a good trumpeter' was certainly applied to someone who smelled badly, but the reference was to bad breath rather than smells from elsewhere.

Tom D'Urfey, the cheerfully scurrilous poet, song-writer and friend to everyone, including Charles II and James II, published his *Pills to Purge Melancholy* in 1719. It includes a comment on:

> She who doth trump,
> Through defect in her rump.

By coincidence, another woman who was 'always trumping' in public places is mentioned in Andrew Wyntoun's *Chronicle of Scotland* (1425). Wyntoun says reprovingly that the woman brought disgrace upon herself in this way.

Twain, Mark

Mark Twain amused himself with the subject of farting, amongst other things, in his *1601*, a privately printed pamphlet which bore the subtitle 'Conversation, as it was by the Social Fireside, in the Time of the Tudors'. The bawdy text, in which Elizabeth I supposedly asks the assembled company who was responsible for the fart which has yielded 'an exceeding mightie and distressfull stink', is readily available on the Internet. See also *Fundamental sigh*.

Ultimate politeness

Khushwant Singh, in *Delhi, a Novel* suggests that the man with the most noble attitude to a female breaker of wind was Sufi Abdul Rahman Hatam Ibn Unwan al assam of Balkh, known as Hatam the Deaf. One day, while the Sufi (a Muslim mystic) was explaining a matter of some theological importance to an old woman, she broke wind. To cover her embarrassment, the Sufi immediately raised his voice and asked her to speak louder because he was hard of hearing. The woman lived another fifteen years, during which time the Sufi kept up his pretence of being rather deaf and allowed people to shout into his ears.

Charles Boewe points out that 'this is a parody of a Persian folk hero, Hatam Tai, famous for his hospitality, who let no passer-by continue his journey until he had been fed. There are restaurants in Iran with names like "Hatam Tai's Place".'

Upper-class farting

In theory, farting makes a nonsense of the social-class system, since it is practised at all levels. J.P. Donleavy, however, has claimed that an inequality exists, even in this activity: 'The upper classes can, with their caviare fed pungencies, knock hell out of the cabbage-stuffed commoner herd.'

Useful farts

A correspondent points out that a fart can at times serve a useful secondary purpose. In a crowded subway train in the rush-hour, a smelly fart can clear a space and make a seat available. As it happens, the New York subway is said to be especially popular with farters. The rattle of a train at speed effectively drowns the embarrassing noise of the average fart, making it impossible to identify the guilty party.

Valentino, Rudolph
· ·

It is part of theatrical legend that Rudolph Valentino, the great
screen lover of the early 1920s, suffered from flatulence. The
fact was mentioned one day on the set of *Carry On Up The
Khyber*, when Kenneth Williams – as the Khazi of Kalabar – was
rehearsing a love-scene with Joan Sims – Lady Ruff-Diamond.
Williams says in his diary entry for 3 May 1968: 'I farted very

loudly and she got up crying out "Pooh! It's disgusting. I can't sit here with this going on – the dirty sod!"' Williams then reminded her that 'Valentino used to blow off.' Gerald Thomas, the director, interposed to say: 'Yes, but they were *silent* films.' This is Williams's own version of the story, recorded in *The Kenneth Williams Diaries*, Russell Davies (ed.). Ned Sherrin, in his *Theatrical Anecdotes*, attributes the punchline to Joan Sims.

Vapour choke

A British slang term for an emission which smells so vile that it chokes anyone in range, other than the perpetrator. 'Vapourize' is occasionally used as a synonym of 'break wind'.

Vater

Vater 'father' is one of the first words that English school-children come across when they start to learn German. Since the word sounds to them like 'farter', it usually causes much hilarity. Many think that 'farter' would in any case be an adequate translation of *Vater*.

Vent

To 'vent' is used in some families to mean 'fart'. The allusion is presumably to the venting of a cask from which gas must be released. Sir John Harington used 'vent' as a noun when he translated a Latin verse of Sir Thomas More:

> To break a little wind
> Sometimes one's life doth save
> For want of vent behind
> Some folk their ruin have.

Ventosity

The preferred word in the sixteenth century for what we now call flatulence. The meaning of 'ventosity' was then extended to include whatever it is in certain foods that produces flatulence. Occasionally the word was used of an actual fart, as in a text of 1568 which refers to 'a stinking ventosity'.

Associated with 'ventosity' and its alternative form 'ventoseness' was the adjective 'ventose'. This meant 'windy' in the flatulent sense, as well as 'puffed up' in the modern sense of a speaker who is said to be 'full of wind'. The latter might be described in modern times as perpetrating 'verbal flatulence'.

Versified farting

A doggerel verse known to many English schoolchildren runs:

> A fart's a volcanic eruption
> That comes from the island of bum,
> It breaks through a barrier of trousers
> And ends with a musical hum.

Vesser

This is one of a group of French words derived from Latin *visire*. *Une vesse*, according to *Le Petit Larousse*, is 'a silent passing of wind through the anus'. *Vesser* is the associated verb, meaning to 'fart silently'. *Un vesseur* is a man who farts frequently in this way, while *une vesseuse* is a French female farter. There is also *une vesse de loup*, literally 'a wolf's fart', which is a kind of mushroom. When Hollyband published his *Treasures of the French Tongue* in 1580, one of the 'treasures' was *c'est un gros [grand] vesseur* – 'he's a great farter.'

Vocative farts

'You fart', 'you old fart' and the like ('you twisted little fart' occurs in *St Urbain's Horseman*, by Mordecai Richler) are normally insulting terms of address, but like all insults they can become covert endearments if spoken in a particular tone of voice between intimates. 'Fart face', especially, is probably to be equated with 'pudding face, fat face, fish face, pie face, funny face and monkey face', all of which tend to display affection rather than animosity. 'You old poop' is reportedly an American variant of 'you old fart'.

Warnings

Some considerate men offer a friendly warning to their colleagues if they are about to contribute an emission of anal gas to the proceedings. 'Wait for it!' is a typical utterance, sometimes accompanied by a slight raising of one leg and a finger held aloft. 'I'd move upwind if I were you' is another possible comment. Mike Shupp reports from California that 'someone about to break wind in company may announce the fact beforehand with "Gas attack"!' A student in Ohio says that a visual as well as verbal warning should be given of an impending fart. 'Cross your index and middle fingers on both hands and say, "Contact!"' The allusion, presumably, is to the instruction given to a pilot to start his engines. Reactions to such helpful remarks and signs tend to vary from 'bloody hell!' to 'you dirty bugger!'

Whales

The Australian marine biologist Richard Martin, who lives in British Columbia, Canada, has written on the topic of whether whales suffer from flatulence, or as he expressed it: 'what wind through yonder humpback breaks?' He was answering a question posed by Kevin Morrison, of Cincinnati, who had

been reading a Tom Clancy novel *Debt of Honor*. There he had found the comment: 'The nervous state of the formation was manifested by the way a frigate five miles out increased speed and turned sharply left, her sonar undoubtedly pinging away now, probably at nothing more than the excited imagination of a sonarman third-class who might or might not have heard a whale fart.' Mr Morrison wanted to know whether whales really do pass gas.

Richard Martin's answer was an emphatic yes. He thought that whales probably deserved a mention in the *Guinness Book of World Records* as the most flatulent creatures in existence, though to his knowledge 'no direct research has been done on whale farts'. Nor was Mr Martin able to make a comparison with the whales' closest land-dwelling relatives, hippopotamuses. Both hippos and whales, it seems, have a three-chambered stomach, but 'unfortunately, no one seems to have studied hippo farts, either.'

Mr Martin then went on to calculate how much gas whales produce. Basing his calculation on the average body weight of nine species of whale and the latest minimum population estimates for those species, Mr Martin suggested that 'the total fart volume generated by whales each day is 455,845,250 quarts. That works out to about 40 billion gallons of fart gas discharged by whales every year.'

These are merely facts and figures. Mr Martin preferred to read a deeper significance into the fact that whales flatulate. 'Our species tends to see itself as something unique and thus apart from nature. But this is an illusion. We are fundamentally linked with our fellow creatures by ancestry and ecology. Farting – like nursing your young, frolicking in the waves, touching bodies out of affection – is another of those intimate acts that we mammals share.' Knowing that whales fart, said Mr Martin, 'helps bring them closer to us'.

Whiffer

A synonym for 'fart' in occasional use, with 'whiff' and 'whiffle' as variants. One meaning of 'whiff' is 'a slight puff of gas', so that 'somebody just whiffed' is often a technically accurate statement. In British slang, something which is 'whiffy' has a bad smell.

Whoof

L. Lane's *ABZ of Scouse* (1966) has an entry: 'Whoof, to pass wind.'

Whoopi Goldberg

The American actress Whoopi Goldberg has a chapter on farting in her autobiography, *Book*. She explains there that her friends started to call her *Whoopi* because she farted so frequently. 'I was like a walking whoopee cushion.' Miss Goldberg adds: 'I always call my farts tree monkeys, 'cause tree monkeys make the same farty sound as I do.'

Wind

'Wind' is frequently used to mean 'gas, flatus', especially in the euphemistic phrase 'break wind'. The word can also be used on its own, spoken apologetically and perhaps with an accompanying tap of the stomach, as an excuse for farting. Someone who is suffering from flatulence might also be described as 'windy'. In theory 'wind' in this sense has no plural form, but there are those who speak about 'having the windies'. To 'make wind' and 'bust wind' are occasionally used instead of 'break wind', while a fart itself can be a 'winder'.

Yachtsmen are sometimes heard to say things like: 'she's got a lot of windage.' They are usually talking about a boat that has a high superstructure rather than a flatulent female acquaintance.

Wind Breaks

The title of a book, by gastroenterologist Professor Terry Bolin and nutritionist Rosemary Stanton, about intestinal gas. By 1995 it was in its third printing.

Windiness

Formerly used to mean 'tendency to cause flatulence'. An early eighteenth-century comment on ginger said that it 'renders cider brisk, and corrects its windiness'.

Wit and judgment

As an illustration of Laurence Sterne's whimsical literary style in *Tristram Shandy*, it would be difficult to find something more typical than his comment: 'Wit and judgment in this world never go together; inasmuch as they are two operations differing from each other as wide as east from west – So, says Locke – so are farting and hiccuping, say I. But in answer to this, Didius the great church lawyer, in his code *de fartendi et illustrandi fallaciis*, doth maintain and make fully appear, that an illustration is no argument.'

Wolf fart

Lycoperdon bovista is the botanical name of the puff-ball fungus which, when dry, emits a cloud of brown spores if you step on it. *Lycoperdon* is a learned translation, credited to the Dutch botanist C.H. Persoon, of 'wolf fist', a dialectal name for the puff-ball. (For 'fist' meaning 'fart', see *Fyst*.) In other regions the puffball is known as 'bull-fist' or 'puff-fist', where again there is a down-to-earth reference to its smell. A seventeenth-century writer remarks on 'that uncleanly mushroom ball which in some countries we a puff-foyst call'.

World-wide flatulence

The appeal of farts and farting is demonstrated by the number of sites dealing with these topics on the Web. The quality of what is on offer varies greatly, and partly depends on the word one searches for, but there is something for everyone. Humour, in fact, plays a large part in the whole operation, and a great many sites are devoted to fart jokes and limericks.

Modern technology also makes it possible to hear many actual or simulated farts. 'Evil Bob', for example, makes available recordings of what he calls his Chili Nonchalant, Forceful and Proud, Perturbed, Zipper, Call of the Wild, Wait for It, Hearty Robust, Mud Sputter, Triple Growler, Barky, Creak 'n Rip, Sneezer and Throat Clearing, to name but a few.

A site called 'Divine Wind' offers instead 'flatulence of the rich and famous', supposedly the anal out-pourings of well-known people. This page does at least state that it is trying to be funny: many of the bizarre offerings on the Web leave the visitor in doubt as to what is intended. There is, for instance, the web page that describes 'the Divine Flatulence Creation Theory'. This maintains that since 'the universe's behaviour can be likened to that of a gas, constantly expanding to fill its container', and it is not known where this gas came from in the first place, it may have begun as the fart of some divine creature.

Worst boss in America

Being 'gassy' was one of the qualities that won the award of America's Worst Boss of 1996 for an office supervisor. His identity was kept secret, since the employee who described him wished to continue working for the company. This was just as well for the boss, since apart from being flatulent, he was also said to be a sexist slob and a cheater.

The survey to find Mr Nasty was conducted by Jim Miller, an expert in management techniques. The winning nomination was submitted in the form of a spoof advertisement for the post of office manager. This stated that the 'successful candidate must be able to schedule fake business trips to spend time with another woman, forcibly kiss his secretary on the lips, wear the same clothes all week, cough in employees' faces, and pass gas and act as though this is normal behavior.'

Wumba

A well-known joke in medical circles concerns a midwife who overhears two African doctors talking when she goes into the hospital staff-room. 'It's wumba,' the first doctor is saying, 'W-U-M-B-A.' 'No,' says the second doctor, 'it's woombaa, W-O-O-M-B-A-A.' 'Wumba,' insists the first doctor. The argument continues in this manner for some time and the midwife decides to intervene. 'I think you'll find, gentlemen,' she says, 'that the word you want is womb, W-O-M-B.' The two doctors look at her blankly for a moment, then one of them says to her: 'Madam, have you ever actually seen a water buffalo?' The second doctor adds: 'And have you ever *heard* one fart in a mudpool?'

You could hear a flea fart

This is an unusual variant on the 'You could hear a pin drop' theme. J.P. Donleavy makes use of it in his story *The Beastly Beatitudes of Balthazar B*: 'You know Balthazar, the wind stopped, the trees were still. You could hear a flea fart.' Emma Lindsey, in an *Observer* article, May 1997, refers to the silence of the audience at a snooker championship by saying that it is 'so quiet you could hear a mouse fart.'

Appendix 1

Euphemisms and Synonyms

The following words and phrases are euphemisms and synonyms for 'fart' mentioned in the A–Z section of this book.

(a) This first section deals with the act of breaking wind, though many of these words and expressions, like 'fart' itself, can occur as nouns as well as verbs.

Back-talk
backfire
bang
bark
beef
beep
belch
belch in reverse
belch upside down
blast away
bleep
blow
blow a breezer
blow a gasket
blow it up
blow off
blow off at the
    bung-hole
blow off steam
blow one
blow one's wind
blowout
blow the horn
blow your horn
blurt
bounce

break company
break gas
break off
break tater
break wind
break wind
    backwards
breeze
brew
bugle
burn bad powder
burp
burst
burst at the
    broadside
bust wind
clap one's cheeks
clear the nether
    throat
compress air
cough
cough in your
    rompers
crack
crack a rat
crack off

crank
crepitate
cut a fart
cut a melon
cut one
cut one loose
cut the Brie
cut the cheese
cut the deck
cut the mustard
deal the blow
dial a traf
dispel air
down wind
drop a bomb
drop a bundle
drop a few
drop a rose
drop one
drop one's guts
drop one's handbag
drop the bomb
drop your lunch
eliminate gas
escape
exhaust air

expel
expel air
expel flatus
expel gas
explode
fart a blue streak
fart off
feist
fib
fice
fire flatus
fist
fizzle
flatulate
float an air biscuit
float an air cake
fluff
fluff your pinky
fogo
foist
foyse
frappe
frog jumps in the
    pond
fumigate
funk
fyst
gas off
go off
grunt
gurk
have air
have an accident
have gas
have the bangs
have the farts
have the heaves
have the windies

honk
horse
kill the Easter
    bunny
kwatz
lay a fart
lay heat
lay one
leave gas
let a brewer's fart
let a crack
let a fart
let a poop
let a scape
let a slipper
let a squib
let a stinker
let a stinko
let a windy
let air off
let an escape
let flee a fart
let gas
let go
let it go
let it out
let it rip
let loose the nether
    zephyr
let off
let off air
let off some gas
let off some wind
let off steam
let one
let one fly
let one go
let one loose

let one off
let one rip
let one slip out
let one's air go
let out air
let out steam
let wind
lift a leg
light it up
lose one's manners
make a bean noise
make a rude noise
make a smell
make bubbles
make gas
make wind
mash a frog
ming
mink
open the lunchbox
pass air
pass gas
pass wind
poop
poot
poot a blue streak
pop
pop a cap
pop a whiff
pop off
prump
puff
punt
push gas
putt
putt-putt
putz
queef

rax
rift
rip one
rip one off
rip your pants
rosepetal
rumble
shoot a bunny
shoot a cricket
shoot a duck
shoot a fairy
shoot Germans
shoot rabbits

sing a hymn
sit on a frog and
    the frog croaks
smell
snort
sound
sound off
spell air
spit it out
spoot
squeak a breeze
squeeze the cheese
step on a duck

step on a frog
stink
take an air dump
talk German
tear air
tee off
thump
toot
trump
vapourize
vent
whiff
whoof

(b) The following words and phrases can replace the noun 'fart' or refer to flatulation in a general way.

afterburner
anal emission
anal exhalation
baked bean blast
barking spider
beanie
beef-heart
belch that's gone
    astray
big blow
blockbuster
bomb
boomer
boop
bottom burp
botty banger
bowel howl
braff
breezer
Bronx cheer

buck snort
buck snorter
bullock's heart
buncil
burnt cheese
butt blast
butt explosion
butt sneeze
cabbage fart
cedar burp
cheek flapper
cheezer
chocolate thunder
clanger
classic fart
crepitation
crepitus ventris
easy slider
episode
event

exhalation
explosion
fart blossom
fartick
fartkin
fire-cracker
flatulation
flatus
flatus incident
fowkin
fritty
gas getting loose
gas in the bowels
gas on the (your)
    stomach
gastric distress
giggle downunder
grime bubble
heart and dart
hinder blast

intestinal utterance
mega-fart
mighty morphin'
    power rauncher
multipopper
ninja fart
noise
pardon
pet
phewy
pocket thunder
poop fume
poopie
pooter
popper
pungency
query
raspberry
raspberry tart
rattler
report from the
    interior
ripper

rolling stomach
roll of thunder
room-clearer
rouser
rude noise
SBD (silent
    but deadly/
    dangerous)
scotch warming-
    pan
silent but violent
silent killer
slider
smelly
snapper
sneaky one
spider bark
squeaker
squeezer
stealth bomber
stench
stewart
stink bomb

stinker
stinky
sweet 'n' low
sweet smell
    of success
tail shot
thumper
tiparillo
Tom Tart
tootle
torpedo
traf
tree monkey
trodden-on frog
trouser cough
under thunder
vapour choke
water bubble
wet one
whiffer
whiffle
winder
windy pop

Appendix 2

Limericks and Jokes

The following flatulent limericks and jokes are mostly in extremely bad taste. Perhaps the only thing in their favour is that they are about one of the few subjects not yet outlawed by the ultra-sensitive politically correct lobby. Breaking wind is not a racial issue, nor does it especially target women, or the old, or the disabled, or the thin or those who are 'larger than average'. Fart humour is simply earthy.

LIMERICKS

A great many anonymous limericks exist which make some reference to breaking wind. Peter Furze was reluctant to include any of them in his thesis (see *Preface* and *Acknowledgments*), even though he methodically collected them as he collected everything else to do with his subject. To some extent Peter's reluctance is understandable. Limericks would not normally come within the scope of an academic enquiry. They have acquired a bad reputation and tend to set up certain expectations. Limerick writers have themselves commented on the situation. One of them remarks:

> A bather whose clothing was strewed
> By winds, that left her quite nude,
> Saw a man come along,
> And, unless I'm quite wrong,
> You expected this line to be rude.

Others have said:

> The limerick packs laughs anatomical
> Into space that is quite economical,
> But the good ones I've seen
> So seldom are clean,
> And the clean ones so seldom are comical.

The limerick's callous and crude,
Its morals distressingly lewd;
    It's not worth the reading
    By persons of breeding
Or anyone else who's a prude.

So there we are – but I felt that it would be wrong to ignore flatulent limericks completely. I have therefore provided a small selection of the genre below. The acknowledged classic in this field is the seven verse effort:

There was a young fellow from Sparta
A really magnificent farter.
    On the strength of one bean,
    He'd fart 'God Save the Queen'
Or Beethoven's 'Moonlight Sonata'.

He could vary, with proper persuasion
His fart to suit any occasion.
    He could fart like a flute,
    Like a lark, like a lute,
This highly fartistic Caucasian.

He'd fart a gavotte for a starter,
And fizzle a fine serenata.
    He could play on his anus
    The 'Coriolanus'
Ooof boom, er-tum, tootle, hum ta-dah.

He was great in the 'Christmas Cantata'
He could double-stop the 'Toccata'
    He could boom from his ass
    Bach's 'B-Minor Mass'
And in counterpoint, 'La Traviata'.

Spurred on by a very high wager
With an envious German named Bager,
    He proceeded to fart
    The whole oboe part
Of the Haydn 'Octet in B-Major'.

It went off in capital style,
And he farted it through with a smile.
    Then, feeling quite jolly,
    He tried the finale,
Blowing double-stopped farts all the while.

The selection was tough, I admit,
But it did not dismay him one bit,
    'Til, with ass thrown aloft,
    He suddenly coughed
And collapsed in a shower of shit.

Here are some less ambitious specimens:

There was a young lady named Cager
Who, as the result of a wager
    Consented to fart
    The whole oboe part
Of Mozart's 'Quartet in F Major'.

Said a printer pretending to wit:
'There are certain bad words we omit.
    It would sully our art
    To print the word f–rt,
And we never, oh, never, say sh–t'

There was a young Royal Marine,
Who tried to fart 'God save the Queen'.
    When he reached the soprano
    Out came the guano
And his breeches weren't fit to be seen.

There was a young man of Australia,
Who painted his bum like a dahlia.
    The drawing was fine,
    The colour divine,
The scent – ah! that was a failure.

There was a young lady named Skinner,
Who dreamt that her lover was in her.
    She woke with a start,
    And let a loud fart,
Which was followed by luncheon and dinner.

I dined with the Duchess of Lee,
Who asked: 'Do you fart when you pee?'
    I said with some wit:
    'Do you belch when you shit?'
And felt it was one up to me.

There was a young lady of Dexter
Whose husband exceedingly vexed her,
    For whenever they'd start
    He'd invariably fart
With a blast that damn nearly unsexed her.

There was a young girl of La Plata
Who was widely renowned as a farter
    Her deafening reports
    At the Argentine sports
Made her much in demand as a starter.

I sat next to the Duchess at tea;
It was just as I feared it would be;
    Her rumblings abdominal
    Were truly phenomenal,
And everyone thought it was me!

There was a young fellow named Charteris
Put his hand where his young lady's garter is.
She said: 'I don't mind,
Up higher you'll find
The place where my pisser and farter is.'

When energy crises arise
We'll scrimp like the cook sage and wise
    Who connected her ass
    To her stove which burned gas
And exploited her farts to make pies.

There was a young man of Rangoon
Whose farts could be heard on the Moon
    When you'd least expect 'em
    They'd burst from his rectum
With the force of a raging typhoon.

There was a young man named McBride
Who could fart whenever he tried
    In a contest he blew
    Two thousand and two
And then shit and was disqualified.

There was a young lady from Kent
Who farted wherever she went
    She went to the fair
    And dropped a few there
So they plugged up her ass with cement.

Perhaps we'd better finish this limerick section with something a little more classical:

A flatulent Roman named Titus
Was taken with sudden colitis;
    And the venerable Forum
    Lost most of its quorum
As he farted up half of the situs.

There are several fart jokes which circulate on the World Wide Web in various forms. The following are typical examples:

Blaming the dog

A young man was invited to meet his girl-friend's parents for the first time. He decided to ingratiate himself with them by making a fuss of Rover, the family dog. While he was stroking the animal he felt the need to pass gas. Fortunately, he made no noise, but a foul smell made itself apparent. 'Rover, come here!' said the girl's father, wrinkling up his nose. The young man was greatly relieved, suspecting that he was likely to offend again. 'But it doesn't matter,' he said to himself, 'the dog will get the blame.' He enticed Rover back to his side and began to stroke him. Then, as predicted, he broke wind again. 'Rover, come away!' said the father, as once again a foul smell filled the room.

Time passed, and the young man realized that gas was building up inside him. He was going to have to release a really dreadful emission. He managed to call Rover to his side, but moments later an unbelievably horrible smell pervaded the area around him. 'Rover!' screamed the father, 'come here! Come away before he shits all over you!'

Farting one's guts out

A married couple had lived together for nearly forty years. The only thing that threatened to come between them in all that time was the husband's habit of breaking wind every morning immediately after waking. The noise would wake up his wife and the smell would make her eyes water. On countless occasions she pleaded with him to do something about his morning flatulations. He told her that there was nothing he could do about a natural bodily function and that she would just have to put up with it. His wife said there was nothing natural about it at all, and if he didn't stop there would come a day when he would fart his guts out. The husband merely laughed.

Years went by. The wife continued to suffer and the husband continued to dismiss her warnings about farting his guts out. Then, one Thanksgiving morning, the wife rose very early and went downstairs to prepare the family feast. She prepared all the traditional dishes, such as pumpkin pie, and of course there was a large turkey. It was while she was taking out the turkey's innards that the wife had an idea. Smiling to herself, she put the turkey guts into a bowl and quietly went upstairs to the bedroom. Her flatulent husband was still sound asleep. Gently she pulled back the bed-covers, then spread the turkey guts over the sheet, near her husband's posterior. She then replaced the bedclothes and tip-toed back downstairs to finish preparing the family meal.

Some time later the sound of flatulent explosions from upstairs told her that her husband had woken up. Moments later she heard a terrible scream, then the sound of frantic footsteps as her husband ran to the bathroom. The wife laughed aloud. After years of putting up with her husband's morning bombshells she had finally got her revenge. But she controlled her amusement and went upstairs, calling to her husband to ask what was the matter. Muffled cries of 'Nothing, it's all right' came from behind the bathroom door. Five minutes later, her husband emerged, a look of horror in his eyes. The wife began to feel rather sorry for him, and again asked him what was wrong.

'I didn't listen to you,' said the husband. 'All those years you warned me and I didn't listen to you.' 'What do you mean?' said the wife, innocently. 'Well, you always told me that I would end up farting my guts out, and today it finally happened.' The wife was about to put him out of his misery and admit to her prank, but her husband continued: 'But by the grace of God and these two fingers, I think I got 'em all back in.'

'Big chief, no fart.'
The chief of an Indian tribe discovered that he had a problem – he could not expel his intestinal gas. This caused him considerable pain. He called for the medicine man, who said that in this instance the chief might need some white man's medicine. The chief spoke no English, so the medicine man went with him to see the doctor and explained: 'Big chief, no fart.' The doctor understood the problem and handed over 20 pills, saying: 'Give him two of these every hour.'

Next day the medicine man and the chief returned to the doctor's surgery. 'Big chief, no fart,' said the medicine man once again. The doctor was puzzled, but was certain that the pills he prescribed were what was needed. He handed over 50 more of them, saying 'Give these to the chief.'

The following day the medicine man returned alone. 'Where's the chief?' asked the doctor. 'Did you give him the pills? What happened?' The medicine man made an expansive gesture. 'Big fart, no chief,' he said.

Confucius say
Confucius say – Man who farts in church sits in own pew.
Confucius say – He who eats too many prunes, sits on toilet many moons.
Confucius say – Stomach pain often gone with the wind.
Confucius say – Man who eat jellybean farts in technicolour.'

Air freshener
An air freshener salesperson was riding in a lift by herself when she broke wind in a smelly way. Thinking quickly, she took a can of air freshener from her sales kit and sprayed the whole lift. When the lift stopped a man got on, sniffed, and said, 'What on earth is that smell?' 'Pine scented air freshener,' said the woman. 'It smells like someone shit on a Christmas tree,' said the man.

Surprise!
There was a man who was very fond of baked beans, but much as he liked them, he dared not eat them because of the disastrous after-effects. He wanted to spare his wife the smells that would inevitably fill the house if he succumbed to temptation and ate a plateful of beans. After years of abstaining, he was on his way home one year on his birthday when his car broke down across the road from a small roadside diner. The tempting aroma of baked beans wafted across the street. Since it was his birthday, he decided to give himself a treat. He reasoned that, as he was going to have to walk home, the effects of the beans would wear off before he got there. He went across to the diner and gorged himself with the beans he loved so much.

When he arrived home his wife met him at the door with a 'Happy birthday! I have a surprise for you!' and insisted on blindfolding him. She then led him into the dining room and sat him down at the table. At that moment the phone rang in the hall. His wife instructed him not to take the blindfold off while she answered the phone. The man was glad that his wife had left the room, because the beans were having a delayed effect. Sitting at the table, he farted noisily, but with a great sense of relief, then waved his hands in front of him to try to get rid of the pungent smell. A few moments later his wife returned and yelled 'Surprise!' as she removed his blindfold. And surprised he was. Twelve friends and relatives who had come to his surprise birthday party were seated with him around the table, all of them holding their noses.

(The basic idea of this joke resurfaces in Britain in a different form, the central character becoming a girl who has just met a rich young man. He takes her to a party at a luxurious apartment in Mayfair. She is so keen to impress him that she is very nervous. This, together with the curry she now regrets having had for lunch, has a bad effect on her, and she desperately tries to get to the bathroom so that she can give vent to her wind. Unfortunately, the bathroom is much in demand.

At this point the young man suggests that they leave, and escorts her to his Jaguar. He opens the door for her, but has to dash back to the party for something he has forgotten. The girl thanks her lucky stars. With great relief she opens the car window and lets fly a rasping honk. A moment or two later Prince Charming reappears, and apologizes profusely: 'Terribly sorry, darling. I haven't introduced you to Carol and Peter.' He indicates his friends, who are sitting red-faced in the back of the car.)

THE END